Cohen Brothers

Cohen Brothers

THE BIG STORE

ENNIS DAVIS

AND SARAH GOJEKIAN

THE History PRESS

Published by The History Press
Charleston, SC 29403
www.historypress.net

First published 2012

Manufactured in the United States

ISBN 978.1.60949.854.2

Library of Congress CIP data applied for.

Notice: The information in this book is true and complete to the best of our knowledge. It is offered without guarantee on the part of the authors or The History Press. The authors and The History Press disclaim all liability in connection with the use of this book.

Contents

Foreword

For those of us of a certain age, shopping at Cohen Brothers big downtown store was as much a part of growing up in Jacksonville as heading to the beach in August or going to the movies to see the latest Western shoot-'em-up picture on Saturday mornings. (If we weren't going with our parents to one of the new suburban drive-ins, we would take the old Ortega 3 bus to the air-conditioned Florida Theater, if not the Arcade or the Imperial.) Thinking back, I can still recall how impressed I was with Cohens' wonderful open-cage elevators that took us up and down between the different departments, each a fascinating world unto itself, on the building's various floors. Likewise, I have happy memories of running up and down the tightly wound marble staircase of the old Carnage Library, eating after-church Sunday dinners at Morrison's Cafeteria (I can still remember the iced tea and the genial efficiency of the wait staff: "No waiting on the lower level!") and marveling at the specialty shops along Bay Street. The Nautical Supply Company, as I remember it, was a veritable old curiosity shop, filled with strange and wonderful devices that hinted at voyages to foreign countries and mysterious ports of call.

Most of all, I remember what it was like to drive downtown at night with my parents during the Christmas holiday season to take in the lighted streets and storefront displays. The lights, the music and the happy mêlée of shoppers combined to transform the blocks around Cohen Brothers into something that approximated the closing scenes of Frank Capra's *It's a Wonderful Life*. For a child, this was a truly magical experience but one that, sadly, is now lost to anyone born after the early 1980s, when most of the other downtown department stores went away. While today we have a "festival marketplace" on the river, downtown Jacksonville looks anything but festive at Christmas or—save for the wonderful Super Bowl extravaganza of 2005—at very many other times. For this and a host of other reasons, it is difficult to convey to younger people a sense of just how much things have changed.

Seventy years before this unhappy transformation, my maternal grandfather, George B. Yenawine Sr., and his family moved down from Louisville to help open up the Cohen Brothers' new, city block–encompassing store, and he managed the linens and furnishings department there until he passed away in 1952. After first renting a house on Laura Street in Springfield, my grandparents moved to the new, up-and-coming streetcar suburb of Avondale. During this period, my mother and her five siblings virtually grew up at Cohen Brothers, and the Big Store was an important, formative part of their lives. In accord with the fond recollections of others in *Cohen Brothers: The Big Store*, they ate at the Big Store's restaurants, met with their friends at the candy counter and were dutifully watched over by the employees. Looking back, it really was a wonderful life.

By the time I was born just after World War II had ended, Cohen Brothers was still Jacksonville's flagship department store, and it anchored a thriving retail district that included such lively competitors as Furchgott's, Ivey's, Levy's, JCPenney, Rosenblum's, Woolworth's and, later, the big new Sears "Cadillac" store over by the riverfront. This core of concentrated commercial activity, along with its professional offices, restaurants, theaters and hotels, continued to define Jacksonville as a city even as its original port and warehouse facilities migrated eastward and new government buildings took their place. By the early 1960s, the trend toward suburban shopping centers was well underway, but few people imagined that these new retail outposts would one day hasten the end of the traditional downtown. As it happens, I was not living in Jacksonville during the critical transitional years of the 1980s, but there is a bit of family folklore that touches on this. Late in her life, my mother still shopped at the by then renamed May-Cohens stores, but on one particular visit, her credit card was no longer accepted. As the young clerk explained to her, she had apparently not used her card for a long period of time, and thus the computer had purged her name from the list of Cohens' customers. Of course, she was more than welcome to fill out all the required paperwork to apply for a new one. After that, I don't think she ever shopped at Cohens again, and for our family, at least, this truly marked the end of an era.

This scene provides a view of the St. James Building and the northeastern corner of Hemming Park. The St. James Building is four stories high. There are people sitting on backed benches in the park. There are cars, parked at an angle to the street, outside the park. The St. James Building is on the National Register of Historic Places. *Courtesy of the Florida Center for Instructional Technology.*

Personal anecdotes aside, Ennis Davis' engaging and well-researched account of "The Big Store" is much more than just a nostalgic look at an important element of Jacksonville's architectural history, although it succeeds admirably in this respect. The story of the rise, fall and eventual rebirth of the St. James Building is a parable of our changing relationship with our downtown districts and our ambivalent feelings about all that has since come to replace them. Since the death of Cohen Brothers/May-Cohens and the other old-line department stores in Jacksonville's downtown, local residents have enthusiastically embraced the culture of happy motoring with its shopping malls, strip centers and Edge Cities. Unfortunately, there is little consensus with respect to how much actual progress has been made in terms of how people work, shop and conduct their lives.

In telling the story of how visionary retailers and architects helped create the twentieth-century American department store, *Cohen Brothers: The Big Store* chronicles its development here in Jacksonville and how it literally reshaped the downtown. One of the signature achievements of the New Urbanism movement, in fact, was the rediscovery of the importance of our recursive interactions with the built environment, even if we are mostly unaware of just how much we are affected by it. Viewed in this light, the decline of America's downtowns has radically altered our basic perceptions about what constitutes a normal human landscape, and the trajectory of suburbanization continues apace to transform every aspect of our lives. Shopping, as Mr. Davis' book so ably recounts, has undergone a complex evolution from the downtown retail districts of the 1920s to the strip centers and ubiquitous big box stores of today.

Now, as I recently heard on the news, online retailers are poised to challenge the hegemony of the big box stores, just as today's sprawl-marts began to eclipse the chain department stores of a generation ago. But what does this next step in the evolution of mass marketing portend for the human experience of place and community, and how will people reshape their social interactions in light of this? Or, as James Howard Kunstler suggests in *The Long Emergency* and *Too Much Magic*, are we instead looking at a return to merchandising at a much smaller and more intimate local scale?

Another aspect of this history has to do with the increasingly contentious relationship between employers and their employees. In their own, mostly unregulated era, the Cohen brothers were thought to be very enlightened in the way that they treated those who worked for them. Although they were probably rather paternalistic by current standards, their concern for the welfare of their store associates (before this term had taken on today's Orwellian overtones) was, by all accounts, genuine. Likewise, their bottom line included a thoughtful appreciation of the local community that supported them, a much different approach from the dominant, shareholder equity–centered business model of today. Through their practices and associations, the founders of the Big Store evidenced an understanding that they were an intimate part of the local ecology of commerce, and employee picnics and perquisites were merely one expression of a much broader and deeper concern. Fortunately, the ethical imperative of mutual support within communities has never entirely gone away, as Joseph William Singer reminds us in his book, *The Edges of the Field*. Whether or not such "uncommon decency" will one day return to the world of business is another question for the future.

Finally, the loss of May-Cohens and the other old-line department and specialty stores from Jacksonville's downtown offers a cautionary tale about the limits of planning in an era of rapid social and technological change. While the death of retailing in the city's central core may not have been inevitable, it would be difficult to say what—if any single action—might have prevented its eventual demise. As *Cohen Brothers: The Big Store* recounts this history, the central business district suffered from a death by a thousand cuts, with each successive store closure and industry relocation contributing to the atrophy of the district's life-sustaining social infrastructure. Unfortunately, by the time the full extent of this loss was grasped, the response of Jacksonville's city officials (despite an abundance of consultant studies) always seemed to be a day late and a dollar short, whatever might have been tried. Three decades later, concerned parties are still trying to come up with grand concepts and "magic bullets" to reanimate Jacksonville's downtown, conflating a poorly connected collection of single-use activity zones with the richly diverse urban tapestry that Jane Jacobs has described.

Encouraged by the emergence of the New Urbanism movement, many of us have anticipated that more people would come to recognize the critical importance of creating and/or preserving more functional, culturally sustaining built environments. In this respect, Jacksonville's recent history has been a very mixed bag, with a smattering of significant successes (including its nationally recognized neighborhood preservation movements and the wonderfully executed adaptive reuse of the St. James Building) and a discouraging number of missed opportunities. This book's real importance, therefore, may be in documenting all of the many factors that came together one hundred years ago to create a truly vibrant and successful urban form. If having a sense of place continues to matter, I would like to think that *Cohen Brothers: The Big Store* is not so much the autopsy of a historic community that has passed away but a guidebook for appreciating (and perhaps replicating) the genius loci of its age.

Milt Hays Jr. is a retired planner and Jacksonville native who writes about planning, politics and New Urbanism.

Acknowledgements

Special acknowledgement is extended to the following individuals, organizations and businesses that have served as major resources for the preparation of this book.

Individuals

Royce Bardin
Michael Berry
Linda Bremer
Paul Bremer
Ron Chamblin
John Christian
Steve Congro
Stephen Dare
Mike Dreaden
Mike Field
Dorothy Fletcher
Sarah Gojekian
Milt Hays Jr.
Daniel Herbin

Jennifer Hewett-Apperson
Jerry Higingbotham
Mike Johnson
Drew Kaplan
Arash Kamiar
Hazel Mack
Robert Mann
Autumn Martinage
Joel McEachin
Lauren Swain Mosley
William Nussbaum
Lisa Sheppard
John Sullivan

Organizations and Businesses

Chamblin's Uptown
City of Jacksonville Historic Preservation Office
City of Jacksonville Planning & Development Department
First Coast Section of the Florida Chapter of the American Planning Association
Florida Center for Instructional Technology
Florida East Coast Railway
Florida Times-Union
Jacksonville Business Journal
Jacksonville Historical Society
Jacksonville Magazine
Jacksonville Public Library Special Collections Department
The History Press
Library of Congress
Malls of America
Metro Jacksonville
New York City Landmarks Preservation Commission
State Archives of Florida
Temple Congregation Ahavath Chesed
Transform Jax
University of Florida Architecture and Fine Arts Library

University of Florida George A. Smathers Library
University of North Florida Thomas G. Carpenter Library
Whiteway Corner

Chapter 1

From Germany to America

In considering the social effects of the department store, one is inclined to attach the greatest importance to the contributions which they have made to the transformation in the way of life of the greatest strata of the population, a transformation which will remain the one great social fact of these last 100 years.
—Hrant Pasdermadjian, The Department Store, Its Origins, Evolution and Economics, *1954*

The Cohen brothers would one day be known as Jacksonville's retail sweethearts, pioneers of urban development and founders of one of the oldest and most important businesses in northeast Florida. While brothers Samuel and Morris Cohen established the family business on Jacksonville's Bay Street in 1867 and were later assisted by another brother, Julius, it would be under the leadership and direction of the youngest sibling, Jacob Elias Cohen, that a small, fledgling enterprise would bloom to become one of the region's largest and most successful retailers.

Recognized to be straightforward in his dealings, farsighted in business acumen, a firm believer in his community and an avid golfer, the story of Jacob Cohen and the Big Store's rise to prominence begins four thousand miles east of Jacksonville in Dublin, Ireland. Born on April 1, 1862, Jacob Cohen was the youngest of eight children begat by Elias and Rae (Heyman) Cohen. Elias and Rae Cohen were both natives of Berlin, Germany. Born in 1807, Elias Philip Cohen was in the general merchandise business and found much success in Berlin, where he was known as an exponent of the trade. It

The Big Store's founder, Jacob Cohen. *Courtesy of the Temple Congregation Ahavath Chesed.*

was here he planted the family namesake his sons would one day heir. Elias Cohen's oldest son, Samuel, was born in 1835 in Germany. In 1845, Morris was born in Poland, and in 1855, Julius was born in Scharmbeck, Germany. The family eventually moved to Dublin, Ireland, where youngest child Jacob was born, but left the Emerald Isle to go back to Berlin a short time after. In Berlin, sons Samuel and Morris graduated from the University of Berlin and started their careers in their father's business.

After the Civil War, the Cohen family immigrated to the United States, setting foot on New York City soil to take advantage of opportunities in the city's growing dry goods industry. Dry goods were products such as textiles, ready-to-wear clothing and sundries. In the United States, typical dry goods retailers carried consumer goods that were distinct from those carried by hardware and grocery stores.

While in New York City, the family were active members of the Reformed Jewish Temple and resided at 464 Eighth Avenue. Elias Cohen's new importing business, Cohen Brothers, was located in Tribeca at the southeast corner of the intersection of Franklin and Church Streets. In 1846, Alexander Turney Stewart, one of New York's wealthiest merchants, established the country's first department store, A.T. Stewart, five blocks south. By the 1870s, the neighborhood had transformed into a burgeoning dry goods district. Cohen's business was a leased space at 97 Franklin Street. Named for Benjamin Franklin, Franklin Street had been previously called Sugar Loaf Street in reference to one of the leading industries in the vicinity.

The structure housing Cohen's establishment was an Italianate-style, five-story loft building, with a first-story cast-iron storefront, constructed by Gardner Colby between 1865 and 1867. Prior to the Civil War, Colby had established the Gardner Colby & Company dry goods business in Boston, Massachusetts. During the Civil War, Colby received numerous government contracts for clothing and owned several properties in the Tribeca area. During the time of Elias Cohen's operation, Colby served as the president of the Wisconsin Central Railroad.

The Civil War had been over for two years when brothers Samuel and Morris visited Jacksonville, Florida, and took note of the potential in a struggling port town trying to reconstruct itself from a war-induced depression. German-born, Jewish and now migrants of the North, the fair-skinned Samuel and Morris made the surprising and unconventional resolve to move their dry goods endeavors to postwar Jacksonville in 1867. They sensed a strength in Jacksonville's residents to rebuild and, more so, to

Elias Cohen's dry goods importing business was located in this Italianate-style, five-story building in what is now known as Manhattan's Tribeca District. *Courtesy of Ashkenazy Acquisition.*

survive and decided their future was there. Their dubious presence would prove selfless and empathetic, as the brothers set out to sow a new beginning for Jacksonville to reap.

The city of Jacksonville's visage following the Civil War in 1865 was less than bleak. Its four thousand residents were clearly striving to recover from a sunken economy. Goods and money were scarce, and farms were yet to be reestablished. In addition, the area was still under martial law and described as a "muddy village" with sidewalks still made of wood. Nevertheless, the Cohen brothers saw a business opportunity. The economy wasn't all bad. The local mills did a large and profitable trade, and lines of steamers from Savannah and Charleston resumed their river trips. Furthermore, the ports of Jacksonville and Pensacola were flourishing due to the demand for lumber and forest products to rebuild the war-torn nation's cities.

New to Jacksonville, the fact that the Cohen brothers were neither Christian, southern nor American-born created great suspicion. Nevertheless, they didn't have to peddle their way to the South like the earliest merchants did since their family was already established in the dry goods trade. Thus, Samuel and Morris Cohen opened Cohen Brothers, the Popular Dry Goods House, in 1867 in a small log cabin on Bay Street between Main and Ocean Streets. Initially, the store had one clerk and one errand boy. There, they sold items such as lace, fine fabrics and curtains. Shortly after establishing their new Jacksonville business, Samuel and Morris were joined by another brother, Julius.

Business thrived from opening day, and within two years, the dry goods retailer had relocated to the Baldwin Block at 41 West Bay Street, between Main and Laura Streets, in a building owned by Dr. Abel Seymour Baldwin. Dr. Baldwin had been the chief surgeon of hospitals for Florida throughout the Civil War. On December 19, 1870, a building housing a mattress factory and grain and hay warehouse caught fire and spread to two adjacent buildings. Rapidly, the fire spread several blocks in the Bay and Pine (now Main) Street areas. When all was said and done, the offices of the Florida Union, Columbus Drew's Book Store, the hardware stores of Samuel Birdsey Hubbard and R.T. Masters and the Cohens' log cabin store were destroyed. After the fire, the Cohen brothers reopened a larger space in the reconstructed Baldwin Building when it was completed.

While his older brothers were establishing a new family business in Jacksonville, the younger Jacob Cohen remained in New York with their parents, where he received his education in the city's public school system. Upon graduating high school, he continued his studies by attending night school. In 1875, Elias Cohen retired from his importing business in Tribeca. Coincidentally, this was the year Jacob joined his three older brothers in Jacksonville, at the mere age of thirteen. When Jacob established his home in the city, there was a population of seven thousand residents. By 1878, Samuel Cohen had relocated to Manhattan, New York, to be a buyer for the growing dry goods business. There in New York, Samuel and his wife, Bertha, raised their seven children: Charles, Henry, Irene, Abraham, Louis, Siddny and Blanche Cohen. Morris, then residing at 49 West Forsyth Street, remained in Jacksonville with Julius and Jacob to run the family business.

By the time Jacob Cohen became a Jacksonville resident, the city had become the nation's most popular winter resort, with "The Winter City in Summer Land" serving as its official slogan. Steamboat excursions on the river had become gala affairs. In 1873, even author Harriet Beecher Stowe stated, "No dreamland on earth can be more unearthly in its beauty and glory than the St. Johns in April," after taking a tour of the river in the vicinity of Jacksonville. According to Erastus G. Hill, a gentleman passing through town in 1877, "Jacksonville is the most delightful town I ever saw on such short acquaintance...All the hotels have bands playing in the parks in front of the house and the evening promenades are delightful."

Over time, Jacob Cohen would witness this winter wonderland's population eclipsing 100,000 residents, with himself largely contributing to its solidity.

Chapter 2

Growth and Disaster

By 1880, Jacob, now eighteen years of age, was running the store. Julius aided Jacob, now the foreman, in the undertaking, and the two lived together in an abode on Bay Street. With Samuel already in New York, Morris moved to England, where he became involved in the lace manufacturing business and eventually was credited with introducing Nottingham lace to the United States. Lace is a fabric patterned with open holes in the work, made by machine or by hand. During this era, Nottingham, England, was the heart of the world's lace-manufacturing industry. There, Morris married Minnie Mendel before relocating to New York City in the late 1880s.

Back in Jacksonville, the city's Jewish population had increased to 130, leading to the "Israelites of Jacksonville" meeting to formally charter the Temple Ahavath Chesed in 1882. Julius Cohen was one of the Jewish congregation's charter members, and soon Jacob joined, eventually becoming one of the congregation's largest donors. Today, the temple Congregation Ahavath Chesed still exists in Jacksonville's Southside and is composed of over seven hundred families. With Jacob now in charge of the family's dry goods enterprise, the business had grown to include 20 employees and over $50,000 in retail stock.

Jacob Cohen's importance in the growth of the family business is paramount and would prove to be greater than that of his familial counterparts in terms of recognition and change. His character was said to be marked by keen anticipation, acute knowledge of the value in service and a drive to develop as the city around him did. He established techniques and standards in merchandising that are commonplace today.

Jacob was the first merchant in the South to set "one price"; there would be no more bias in pricing on a customer-by-customer basis. With this, he was the first to put a price tag on his goods. Even more unheard of at the time, in transaction, he initiated the principle of offering refunds to unsatisfied customers. Jacob is said to have been the first to come up with "sale prices" in Florida. And he was the first to give correct change, introducing pennies to Florida. Prior to that time, custom was to make all payment in multiples of five cents. At the time, Jacksonville, as well as the whole state, had no pennies, seemingly because they were only circulating primarily in large cities. Baffled by this deficiency, the brothers would stuff their kit bags full of pennies when traveling from New York City.

Jacob's continued mark on the firm earned him the nickname "The Wanamaker of the South" in reference to retail great John Wanamaker. In 1861, Wanamaker partnered with his brother-in-law, Nathan Brown, to establish Oak Hall, Wanamaker & Brown in Philadelphia, Pennsylvania, three days before the start of the Civil War. By 1871, with sole control, Wanamaker transformed his business into the country's largest men's clothing store, while also becoming the first American retailer to travel overseas to purchase merchandise. By the 1880s, Wanamaker was considered by some to be the father of modern advertising and marketing.

Along with the Cohens' mounting presence marking their dry goods business as a key institution of the city, the mid- to late 1880s saw distinct events that would again change the economy in Jacksonville. Yellow fever swept much of the country as a reoccurring epidemic throughout the nineteenth century. A viral infection spread by mosquitoes, it was known then to attack the organs, make the skin turn yellow and induce "fatal" black vomit. At the time, it was deemed one of the most dangerous infectious diseases. It would continue to fume into the twentieth century along the Atlantic Coast until a vaccine was developed by Max Theiler in 1937.

Jacksonville was most notably hit with the hellish "Jack" in 1888, with the disease seeping into the city on precisely July 28, according to records. Yellow Jack was the personification of yellow fever, a cartoon tycoon of an invisible company designed to overthrow vigor and strip families of health and being. Slapped on newspapers, it was a face everyone knew: "a skeleton shrouded in wispy graveclothes, wearing a yellow sombrero, which indicated his supposed Cuban birthplace." The fever spread uncontrollably in less than two weeks.

Completed at the present intersection of First and Main Streets, the Sub-Tropical exposition's grand opening was attended by President Grover Cleveland in 1888. Intended to be a Florida tourist attraction, its prospects for success failed due to the area's yellow fever epidemics. *Courtesy of the State Archives of Florida.*

The options for reaction were to stay where your home was and face the epidemic or try to flee the city untouched. The latter was near impossible, as guards were set up to seal all exits from the city as a means of quarantine, shotguns in tow. Nevertheless, most residents tried to escape. This led to a compaction of refugees and chaos in transportation outlets. It also led to a physical and metaphorical emptiness in the city. All business and work was suspended, making city government defunct, "the heads having fled." It left the city and its people damned by those in others, as no one wanted to be contaminated by refugees from "that place." Yellow flags marked the homes of the sick, and death carts patrolled nightly collecting the dead. Quarantines grew tighter with set-up camps for detainment, talk of horror stories leaked back with a vengeance and outbound trains and steamboats were being viciously halted and rerouted. The City of Montgomery, Alabama, even offered a cash reward for a captured Jacksonville refugee. Conflicting reasons for the epidemic's cause amounted to the consensus that it was an airborne poison in the form of a gas and that gunpowder and bonfires were the solution, "concussing" the microbes and purifying the atmosphere. There was advice to refrain from eating meat or cabbage, as the cause might be a germ in animal or plant life. Little did they know it was bugs, invisibly swarming about them, much like their grasp of the plague.

An excursion train of the Jacksonville, St. Augustine and Halifax River Railway during the 1880s. Henry Flagler's purchase and extension of this railroad eventually led to the end of Jacksonville's reign as Florida's tourism mecca. On September 7, 1895, the system was renamed the Florida East Coast Railway. *Courtesy of the State Archives of Florida.*

This, however, would be known nearly a dozen years later when Dr. Walter Reed stumbled on the vector while researching in Cuba.

Eventually, a distress call was answered by others, their sympathy sinking in. The American Red Cross dispatched nurses to Jacksonville for nearly three months—nurses who had to jump from the moving train that wouldn't stop in the city for them. Eight of them supposedly died of the fever. Monetary contributions came in, and cities lent even more artillery to help "blast" the air. People carried on any way they could. One story reports two men "vaccinating" themselves with six bottles of champagne; they didn't know if they had the fever or not but knew they had very big headaches the next day. Before running its course, yellow fever afflicted 4,656 of the 14,000 people left in the city, killing more than 400, including the city's mayor, C.B. Smith. The epidemic finally ended on November 25, 1888, when the temperature fell to a chilly thirty-two degrees Fahrenheit and the cold was really able to "blast" the mosquitoes.

In 1883, American tycoon Henry Morrison Flagler visited St. Augustine with his new bride, Ida Alice Shourds. Despite finding area hotel facilities inadequate, the partner of John D. Rockefeller in Standard Oil fell in love with the area and soon began building the 540-room Ponce de Leon Hotel. Now Flagler College, the Ponce de Leon Hotel opened on January 10, 1888. Realizing he needed a mode of transit for his Florida real estate investments, Flagler purchased the Jacksonville, St. Augustine and Halifax River Railway (JSt.A&HR) on December 31, 1885. By 1889, with the acquisition of the St. John's Railway, the St. Augustine and Palatka Railway and the St. Johns and Halifax River Railway, Flagler's system provided rail service from Jacksonville to Daytona Beach, eventually forming what is now known as the Florida East Coast Railway. On January 5, 1890, Flagler opened a single-track swing bridge over the St. Johns River, connecting his railroad to Jacksonville's Union Station.

Flagler followed the extension of his rail line with the purchase of the Hotel Ormond near Daytona Beach in 1890 and the construction of the Royal Poinciana Hotel in 1894. Located on the shores of Lake Worth in Palm Beach, Florida, the 1,100-room Royal Poinciana Hotel was the largest wooden structure in the world when it was completed. Two years later, Flagler constructed the Palm Beach Inn overlooking the Atlantic Ocean. The Palm Beach Inn was renamed the Breakers Hotel in 1901.

Despite Flagler's extension of the railroad south of the St. Johns River, Jacksonville rebounded from the yellow fever outbreaks of the previous decade, rebuilding its status as a winter resort and tourism mecca. This economic resurgence would be short-lived, as a series of freezes in 1894 hit the city and most of the state. Prior to this, Flagler's intention was to extend his railroad system south, terminating in the city of West Palm Beach. However, upon finding it, too, was hit by the freezes, he settled on a town sixty miles south that was apparently unaffected, known today as Miami. Several landowners in the town were intrigued by this possibility, and to help convince Flagler to extend it there, they offered land in exchange for laying tracks. One such owner was Julia Tuttle. Tuttle ran a trading post on the Miami River, the Florida East Coast Canal and Transportation Company. In her request to Flagler, Tuttle sent him a twig from her orange tree with a white blossom on it. The original owner of the land, she is credited for cultivating the city of Miami.

Despite the volatile economy, Jacksonville increased in population 124.8 percent, growing from 7,650 residents in 1880 to 17,201 by 1890, surpassing Pensacola to become Florida's largest city. As a result, in 1897, the Cohen Brothers, the Popular Dry Goods House, moved to larger quarters. Its new address at 29–33 West Bay Street was the newly opened Gardner Building, between Main and Laura Streets. The six-story building was Jacksonville's first skyscraper and the tallest in the state of Florida. Cohen Brothers occupied the entire first and second floors. From the entrance in the center of the store could be seen an elaborate display of retail rebirth. Nearly eight thousand square feet of products was dominated by great show windows that extended around to the elevator and stair lobby. The interior was made of a duo of polished oak and mirrors. According to Jacob Cohen, "The ladies of Jacksonville required more correct style and more up-to-date methods, so they got goods at the same figures as retailed in New York."

Jacob again brought about new ways of conducting business, this time relating to the vigor of his employees. New conveniences for female employees included modern stools used for resting between customers, designated toilet rooms and supplied writing desks and paper. Instead of using cash carriers, a device that would carry customers' payments from sales assistants to cashiers and the change and receipt back again, they used cash boys so the boys would have employment. Many of the hired boys—who would go on to hold high positions in Cohen Brothers—were poor and needy of work, and Jacob saw them worthy of it. His interest in human aid was never quite made public, as he shied from the limelight. Other concerns shortened workdays for thousands of workers. The Cohen brothers pioneered the early closing movement, as stores had before opened at dawn and gone on to see dusk before closing shop. They declared Saturday hours to be the same as weekdays. They also provided night schooling for boys who could not attend school due to work during the week.

The late 1880s and 1890s were also a period of ups and downs for the Cohen family. On September 6, 1887, Jacob Cohen married Hattie Halle. Over the next decade, five children were born to the newlyweds—Edna in 1888, Halle in 1893, Rae in 1895, Hazel in 1897 and Minna in 1899. However, Jacob's older brother Julius died in Jacksonville in 1891 at the age of thirty-eight of typhoid fever. That same year, the Cohen brothers' father, Elias Philip Cohen, passed away at the age of seventy-five in New York City. Five years later, Rae, his widow, died at the age of sixty in 1896.

By 1900, Jacksonville had grown 65.3 percent since 1890 and had a population of 28,429. However, on May 3, 1901, an event took place that would forever change the direction and impact of Cohen Brothers on the city of Jacksonville's development patterns. At 12:30 p.m., a small fire began at the Cleveland Fibre mattress factory, which was located northwest of downtown Jacksonville at the intersection of Beaver and Davis Streets. Initially, when the fire was discovered, workers attempted to put it out with a few buckets of water. Unable to control the growing blaze, the fire department

A portrait of young cash boys and wrappers at Cohen's Bay Street competitor, Furchgott's. All under the age of twelve and one as young as nine, they worked for three dollars a week. *Courtesy of the Library of Congress.*

The remains of Cohen Brothers, the Popular Dry Goods Store, and the Gardner Building after the Great Fire of 1901, rise in the background of the H. & W.B. Drew Company building. *Courtesy of the State Archives of Florida.*

was then alarmed. However, by the time the fire department arrived, the fire had already begun to consume nearby wood-frame structures. Within a few minutes, the inferno rapidly spread east, consuming everything in its path, including Cohen Brothers' new dry goods store on Bay Street. Eventually, the natural water bodies of Hogans Creek and the St. Johns River stopped the eastward spread of destruction.

Nevertheless, after eight heartbreaking hours, the fire had consumed 146 city blocks, destroying over two thousand buildings, killing seven and leaving ten thousand Jaxsons—including the Cohens—homeless. It was said that the glow from the flames could be seen in Savannah, Georgia, and smoke plumes as far north as Raleigh, North Carolina. Over the years, this tragic event eventually became known as the Great Fire of 1901, the third-largest urban fire in American history behind the 1906 San Francisco Earthquake and the Chicago Fire of 1871.

Chapter 3

THE BIG STORE COMES TO JACKSONVILLE

Jacob Cohen was in New York on a business trip when the Great Fire of 1901 burned his business to the ground. He found out about this tragic event by coming out of a theater on a late night to discover newspaper headlines claiming Jacksonville had been devastated by fire. With no way of knowing if his family was dead or alive, he returned to Jacksonville. Back in Jacksonville, he learned that his wife and four kids had been rescued in a horse-drawn wagon by Jim Vickery, a family friend. Vickery had also saved the family's silver, while Cohen's eight-year-old son, Halle, ran back for his school books.

Upon returning to Jacksonville, Jacob Cohen became a member of the city's Relief Committee, helping to restore order from the chaos that had come as a result of the devastation. A visionary, Cohen also lobbied that all city streets should be made wider than they were originally.

After the fire, Cohen Brothers, the Popular Dry Goods House, set up a temporary operation in the Acme Building on the northwest corner of Bay and Julia Streets. The store remained in this location until a new two-story version of the Gardner Building was constructed. Due to rapid growth of the business and the urgency for additional space, a third floor was constructed on top of the building. Like Cohens, the city around the dry goods store was rapidly overcoming the devastating fire of 1901. During the first decade of the twentieth century, the city grew at such a pace that 13,000 new buildings had replaced the 2,368 lost in the fire by 1910.

The rebuilt Gardner Building on Bay Street shortly after the completion of the Big Store at Hemming Park. Before the relocation of Cohen Brothers, a third floor had been added to the Gardner Building in the years after the Great Fire of 1901 to accommodate the growing dry goods business. *Courtesy of the City of Jacksonville Historic Preservation Office.*

Looking west at the intersection of Bay and Main Streets with Cohen Brothers, the Popular Dry Goods Store, in the background. During the first decade of the twentieth century, Bay Street was the epicenter of Jacksonville's commercial district. The Cohens' decision to relocate to Hemming Park was considered a risky proposition at the time. *Courtesy of the Library of Congress.*

With the rapid growth of the rebuilding city centered on innovation, enlightenment and creativity, the atmosphere presented Jacob Cohen with an opportunity to do something greater than most in Jacksonville would ever imagine: build a full-line department store on the abandoned site of the St. James Hotel, several blocks north of Jacksonville's established retail district along Bay Street. The St. James Hotel for many years had been one of the most famous hotels in the South and was the mecca of Florida tourism. Shortly after the Civil War, northern capitalists decided to construct one of the most elegant hotels of the South in Jacksonville on this site overlooking Hemming Park. The hotel opened to the public on January 1, 1869, and consisted of four stories, accommodating five hundred guests. Prominent guests of the era, including presidents of the United States, enjoyed the hotel's grand ballrooms, which were said to ring nightly with the dance music of the period. J.R. Campbell was the hotel's proprietor for all thirty-two years of its operation. The grand hotel's last day in business was May 3, 1901, the day of the Great Fire of 1901, which destroyed the building.

Adjacent to the St. James Hotel was the Windsor Hotel. The Windsor Hotel was known as one of the most comfortable and homelike hotels in the United States after it opened in 1875. Standing three stories tall, the sprawling, gingerbread-frosted wooden structure accommodated four hundred guests at its Hogan Street location, which overlooked Hemming Park's west border. At the time of its opening, Hemming Park was filled with tropical trees and plants and surrounded by magnificent oaks and orange trees. When the structure burned down as a result of the Great Fire of 1901, it would be the only grand hotel of nineteenth-century downtown Jacksonville to be rebuilt. However, instead of wood, its proprietors, Dodge and Cullis, erected the new structure of brick, stone and steel in the Spanish Renaissance architectural style. Several organizations were developed in the hotel's community rooms and on its colonnade facing Hemming Park. Among these were the Women's Club of Jacksonville, which held its first meeting at the hotel in 1897; the Jacksonville Rotary Club in 1912; and eventually the Kappa Kappa Gamma sorority, which formed its Alumni Association at the Windsor in 1942. Lee Bigelow, in his *History of Jacksonville*, tells what it was like to spend a day at the Windsor:

> *After a breakfast presenting a most varied menu of fruit, fish and game, the first move was generally to the front piazza and a rocking chair while one read the morning mail and newspapers, a little later would come the*

The St. James Hotel prior to the Great Fire of 1901. The hotel was so prominent during the nineteenth century that the public square that would eventually become Hemming Park was renamed St. James Park. *Courtesy of the Library of Congress.*

leisurely stroll down Hogan or Julia Street to Bay, then easterly, generally on the north side as far as Market to the post office and the Carleton Hotel; then back again and perhaps up Pine (Main) to Duval and back to the park, passing en route many curio shops where Florida novelties of all kinds were exposed to tempt the purchaser. It seems as if every visitor to Florida felt compelled to buy something made either of the alligator, or that bore his grotesque likeness. Orange wood canes and fish-scale jewelry were also much in demand...Usually in the forenoons the hotel orchestras, and every tourist hotel had a good one, would play a morning concert on the hotel piazzas or in the park. Then, there was a midday meal of excellent variety, to be followed in the afternoon by a more formally attired dress parade, practically over the same route, or perhaps a drive out in the country over roads that were none too good. After supper every night there was music for dancing in the parlors for all those who desired to indulge in that form of recreation, euchre and other card games, and a billiard room for the gentlemen. Evenings, particularly the moonlight ones, the piazzas were well patronized until about 10:30 or

> *11:00. About once a week the big hotel dining rooms would be cleared after an early supper and a formal ball given, or else the colored waiters would put a Cake-walk, a sort of minstrel-like dance and parade, in which all sorts of fantastic steps were introduced, and the judges, often chosen from the guests, would decide which couple was entitled to receive the most elaborate cake the hotel pastry cook could devise and prepare. Sometimes one hotel would compete with another and the rivalry ran high.*

When it came to the rivalry between the neighboring Windsor and St. James Hotels, the Windsor would ultimately win out. After the fire, the St. James Hotel site remained empty and undeveloped for years, periodically being used by the traveling Gentry Brothers Dog and Pony Show. "The show is larger, better and more pleasing than ever before," said the *Florida Times-Union* in 1902. "Many new features have been added…it is full of bright, sparkling acts and laughable climaxes."

The Windsor Hotel shortly after the completion of the St. James Building and Cohen Brothers' Big Store. A longtime competitor of the St. James Hotel, Windsor Hotel ownership purchased the St. James site after the Great Fire of 1901 to eliminate the possibility of the hotel being rebuilt. *Courtesy of the Library of Congress.*

In 1885, after training a few animals and corralling his three brothers, seventeen-year-old Henry B. Gentry bought a train car and got a show on the road. By 1910, the Bloomington, Indiana–based circus was considered the largest traveling and greatest dog and pony show in the United States, featuring seven elephants and four camels.

During this time, several schemes for new development were proposed, including a six-story hotel designed by architect Henry J. Klutho for proprietor J.R. Campbell in 1904. Like the others, Campbell's project failed to get off the drawing board, resulting in his offering of the property to the city as a public park in March 1906. However, Mayor George M. Nolan declined because he felt the site was better off being used for the development of another hotel instead of a public park. Seizing the opportunity, Frank T. Cullens, one of the owners of the neighboring Windsor, quickly purchased the property a month later for $100,000, with the intent to keep a competing hotel from being developed on the site. In February 1909, a proposal to build an amusement park on the site was announced by the president of the recently organized St. James Amusement Company, W.W. Todd. Just as soon as this project—which would have featured an immense auditorium and 163 booths ranging from a German beer garden to a Japanese pagoda—was announced, Jacksonville residents objected. When this proposal died by the summer of 1909, the city council appointed a committee to study the concept of building a new city hall or auditorium to attract conventions to the city. However, nothing had come to fruition by the time brothers Jacob and Morris Cohen decided to place an offer on the property for $100,000 in February 1910. The Cohens' vision aligned with the desires of the Windsor Hotel's owners, who would only agree to sell the site on the condition that it would not be used for the construction of a competing hotel. The brothers didn't intend to build a hotel. They anticipated the construction of a new store that would become one of the largest buildings and a "game changer" for the city of Jacksonville.

In a quest to expand the family's growing business, Jacob Cohen enlisted financial assistance and advice from David May, an old friend and founder of the May Company. May purchased stock in Cohen Brothers under an agreement by which he later resold it to the store owner. Furthermore, Morris Cohen, who relocated to Nottingham, England, and New York in the 1880s, returned to Jacksonville to help with management, serving as the department store's vice-president until his death in the mid-1920s.

On March 1, 1910, the Cohens selected architect Henry J. Klutho to design their new store, which would be the ninth-largest department store in

Looking at the Bay Street business district from Cohen Brothers, the Popular Dry Goods Store, in 1908. *Courtesy of the State Archives of Florida.*

the United States. Born in Breese, Illinois, in 1873, Klutho attended Schenk's Drawing Academy in St. Louis, Missouri, before moving to New York City in 1894. After a tour of Europe in 1899, he opened his own architectural practice in New York. In 1901, the *New York Times* article informing New Yorkers of Jacksonville's fiery demise that brought concern to Jacob Cohen's heart presented Klutho with the opportunity of a lifetime. Within months of reading about the calamity, Klutho left New York to establish a new office in Jacksonville. Since then, the young architect had quickly become one of Jacksonville's most noted architects, landing several high-profile commissions such as the Dyal-Upchurch Building, the Thomas V. Porter residence, the First Baptist Church Sanctuary, the Jacksonville Free Public Library and the new Jacksonville City Hall.

During a trip to New York in 1904, Klutho met Frank Lloyd Wright. At the time, Wright had two important commissions—the Darwin D. Martin residence and the Larkin Building—underway in Buffalo. Wright was a Chicago-based architect, interior designer, writer and educator who believed that structures should be designed in harmony with humanity and the surrounding environment. In the late nineteenth century, Wright had been mentored by Louis Henry Sullivan while employed at Sullivan's firm, Adler & Sullivan. By the turn of the century, Wright had become the most famed practitioner of an architectural style inspired by Sullivan's Chicago School style, which was distinguished by the inclusion of masonry cladding and large plate-glass windows on steel-frame buildings. Known as Prairie School, its distinguishing design characteristics included horizontal lines, flat or hipped roofs with broad overhanging eaves, windows grouped in horizontal bands, integration with the landscape, craftsmanship and discipline in the use of ornamentation. In addition, sometime between 1904 and 1907, Klutho and his wife, Elizabeth, were guests at Wright's house and studio in Oak Park, Illinois. Wright's works and philosophies appealed to Klutho, whose Jacksonville commissions began to reflect the more modernistic concepts developed by Frank Lloyd Wright and his mentor, Louis Sullivan, by 1907.

After his selection for the St. James project, Klutho traveled to New York with Jacob Cohen to evaluate the most famous and modern stores in preparation for developing a grand structure for the St. James site. Initially, Jacob and Morris Cohen desired a two-story building lined with balconies that would have only been devoted to their store. However, Klutho convinced them that this was an opportunity to create an urban center that did not exist in the South at the time. Instead of a two-story structure, Klutho suggested a four-story, mixed-use building featuring rental apartments on the upper levels.

Excavation work on the site began before the building was fully designed as a cost-cutting measure by Klutho. With the need to remove sand for the site, Klutho offered it for free to anyone willing to remove it. J.A. Ritter ended up accepting Klutho's offer and eventually made a profit selling the sand he removed as fill dirt for other projects.

After the Cohens rejected Klutho's idea of including residential units in the proposed structure, Klutho suggested office use as an alternative. Initially, the Cohens were hesitant because they felt the site, which was two blocks north of Forsyth Street, was too far removed from the core of Jacksonville's business district. Klutho was able to get the Cohens to agree to this mixed-use concept by making the point that New York's business center had moved from 14th and 24th to 34th and north as the city had grown and densified.

During the design process, several design documents were presented to the Cohens. These included several versions of the two-story structure initially desired by the Cohens and one very detailed Prairie School–style version of the four-story alternative envisioned and promoted by Klutho. That scheme

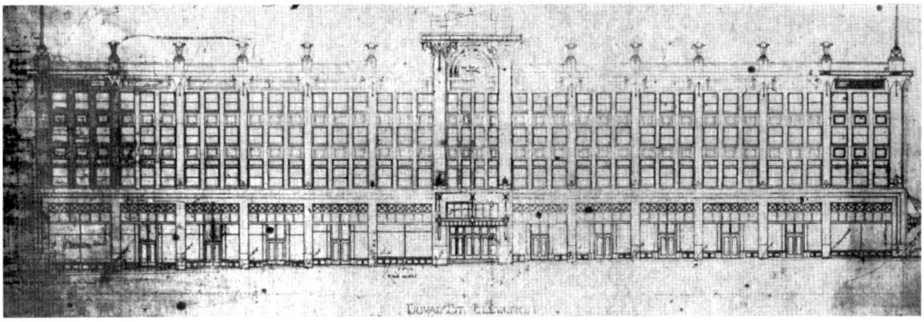

A Duval Street elevation blueprint of Henry J. Klutho's Prairie School–style St. James Building in 1911. *Courtesy of the University of Florida Architecture and Fine Arts Library.*

envisioned the Cohens' department store occupying most of the first floor and all of the second and office space for the third and fourth floors. The remaining square footage of the first floor was reserved for smaller retail shops along West Duval Street, overlooking Hemming Park.

Eventually, Klutho was successful in gaining the Cohens' acceptance to construct an elaborate four-story Prairie School structure overlooking Hemming Park. What had begun as a desire to construct a new department store had evolved into Klutho's single largest commission. In January 1911, a front-page rendering of the project appeared in the *Evening Metropolis* newspaper, providing the public with their first view of the building's design. Estimated to cost $500,000, the project was named after the St. James Hotel that had been lost in the Great Fire of 1901.

With the design of the St. James Building, Klutho was able to successfully blend the principles of Louis Sullivan and Frank Lloyd Wright with his own personal style. His design represented a radical departure from the more traditional architectural styles of the early twentieth century. At the heart of the building was an atrium featuring a seventy-five-foot octagonal glass skylight, intended to flood the interior of the structure with natural light. The skylight included eight sculpted Atlantean figures that appeared to visually support the skylight on their shoulders. A two-ton bronze chandelier with four cascading octagons holding 250 incandescent lights, the second-largest chandelier in the country at the time, was the centerpiece of the glass skylight. Furthermore, the second floor's concrete railings were pierced with geometric openings reflecting the Cohens' Jewish faith and culture. With the front of the building facing the park, freight, packing and employees' facilities were positioned along the structure's Church Street façade, which was one block to the north. With the first floor being twenty feet in height, a small mezzanine

One of eight heroic sculpted figures designed to appear to visually support the Big Store's central skylight on their shoulders. *Courtesy of the City of Jacksonville Historic Preservation Office.*

level was included along the Church Street façade. The third and fourth floors of the St. James Building were designed to form a U, with sixty offices per floor around a center fall for additional tenants. Tying the interior floors together was a system of open elevator cages with cast-bronze geometry resembling the concepts of Frank Lloyd Wright.

On the exterior, the design of the reinforced structure's walls included five hundred linear feet of polished plate-glass store windows and terra cotta capitals with ornamentation resembling the influences of Louis Sullivan's Chicago School concepts. The Conkling-Armstrong Terra Cotta Company of Philadelphia manufactured and shipped the Klutho-designed capitals.

Fitting in with the surrounding urban environment, the building's first floor featured nine individual retail spaces facing Hemming Park, utilizing

The St. James Building central atrium and skylight as it exists today. *Courtesy of the author.*

the park as a garden overview. In addition, following the principle of "form follows function," the Louis Sullivan–influenced central tower facing Hemming Park, which included a cantilevered suspended glass canopy, defined the primary entrance to the Cohens' store, as well as shielded a large water tank behind its raised parapet. In addition to serving as the architect of the St. James Building, Klutho also served as the project's contractor. He received an estimated $40,000 for his services. Using the fast-track method, Klutho was able to complete the construction of the mammoth project within an eighteen-month period.

Recounting his experience on the design and construction of the St. James Building, Klutho would state:

> *Few people realize what it means to design and execute a building of this character. To many it is but a mass of brick and stone studded with windows—built by the masons and carpenters and the result a happy or unhappy accident as the case may be. They realize not that the form and size of it had to be thought out in a man's brain—as it were, a dream;*

> *that the dream had to be made a reality, by being transferred to paper by means of lines. To do this correctly, in a way to be intelligently understood by the artisans, contractors, and workmen that enter into the construction of a building, is a science that is called architecture. Every detail, every projection, every column and girder, every bit of ornament from the cornices down to the picture mould and the massive electric engines to the switch, the rough plumbing pipe to the finished, white glazed fixture has been thought out, figured and outlined months before it is actually put into the building. So accurately, has this to be done that contractors can submit estimates of prices on the cost of these things and are able to make out estimates to the fraction of a penny, by consulting the plans and specifications. In order that the public might know the amount of energy and time consumed in planning such a structure, it might be of interest to know that it has taken an office force of five assistants more than two years to draw these plans. More than 1,500 blueprints were given out to various contractors, and over 250 sheets of drawings were made. Over 3,000 letters have been sent out and received and 350 telegrams exchanged. About twenty-five separate and distinct contracts have been entered into with subcontractors and each provided with a set of plans and specifications, all having reference to this one building.*

The St. James Building had become the Prairie School masterpiece of Henry J. Klutho's architectural career and one of the most distinctive buildings in Jacksonville. Soon after its completion, it became the recipient of national attention and acclaims. In 1914, the building and its architect were featured in *Western Architect*. In 2001, Robert Broward, Kluto's biographer, described the St. James Building as "the most powerful architectural and urban statement in Jacksonville after more than seventy years."

Chapter 4

AN INSTITUTION FOR THE PEOPLE

One of the first things I decided to do when we moved to our new big store was not to buy any other property around or near the new location. I thought it best that if other people bought these locations and built big buildings around our new building it would be much better and help us.
—Jacob Cohen

On Sunday, October 20, 1912, a newspaper advertisement claimed, "The new store is yours. Our rapidly Growing City has made this a public necessity." What Jacob Cohen built was an innovation for marketing and business not only as a new form of retail institution but for all of Jacksonville society. The Big Store affected several facets of social and economic life in Jacksonville. According to Statistics Canada's official definition, a department store must sell at least three different commodity lines such as (1) clothing; (2) furniture, appliances and home furnishings; and (3) others (i.e. cosmetics, jewelry, sporting goods, etc.). No one line can account for more than 50 percent of the store's total sales, and at least 10 percent of the store's sales must come from the third (others) set of lines.

On October 21, at 10:00 a.m., the official grand opening of the St. James Building and the Cohens' "Big Store" took place. Two orchestras, one led by Professor Wilhelm Meyer, entertained the crowd. With the opening of the Big Store, the Cohens added several new departments to their inventory, including books, candy, china, groceries, house furnishings, stationery and a soda fountain in their quest to become a full-line department store. The

The Big Store was well received, drawing over twenty-eight thousand visitors on opening day, October 12, 1912. When it was completed, it was the ninth-largest department store in the country. *Courtesy of the City of Jacksonville Historic Preservation Office.*

Cohens' investment was well received, drawing over twenty-eight thousand visitors on opening day and officially becoming the ninth-largest department store in the nation, covering over 300,000 square feet of retail floor area. The largest department store in the United States was Macy's of New York with over 1 million square feet. According to the *Florida Times-Union* on October 15, 1912, "Cohen Brothers is more than a great towering structure of stone and steel. It is imbued with Life and Energy and Efficiency."

Furthermore, as part of the building's construction, fourteen modern three-thousand-candlepower streetlights, said to be the first and finest south of Baltimore, were also added. Upon completion, it was claimed that this was the brightest illuminated block in the United States. Soon, the city would install a similar lamp design on Adams Street, a full mile from Main Street to Myrtle Avenue.

In addition to the Cohen Brothers Big Store, a number of businesses opened in the newly completed St. James Building, solidifying Jacob

A look at the early soda fountain of Cohen Brothers' Big Store. When the Big Store opened, one of the soda fountain's most popular beverages was Cherry Smash. At the time, the flavorful beverage was called "the most popular soft drink next to Coca Cola." *Courtesy of the Jacksonville Historical Society.*

Cohen's vision of the structure becoming an institution for the people. The first floor of the Prairie School structure featured four street-front retail spaces overlooking Hemming Park. The original tenants of these storefronts included Bettes Pharmacy, St. James Tonsorial Parlor and the Camera & Art Shop. The Camera & Art Shop was a photographers' supply store managed by Harry W. Fagan. Next door to Fagan's shop was Alphonso J. Nadreau's St. James Tonsorial. At 105 Duval Street was pharmacist Charles C. Bettes' pharmacy, which stocked physicians' supplies, toilet articles, cigars and mineral water. Bettes, who had served as a drug clerk in Jacksonville since 1879, had established his pharmacy in 1891. Like Cohen Brothers, Bettes' business had been destroyed in the Great Fire of 1901. He opened a pharmacy at 53 and 55 West Bay Street in 1903 before relocating to the St. James Building. At the time of the building's opening, Bettes and his wife, Laura, resided at 315 East Ashley Street while their new mansion in

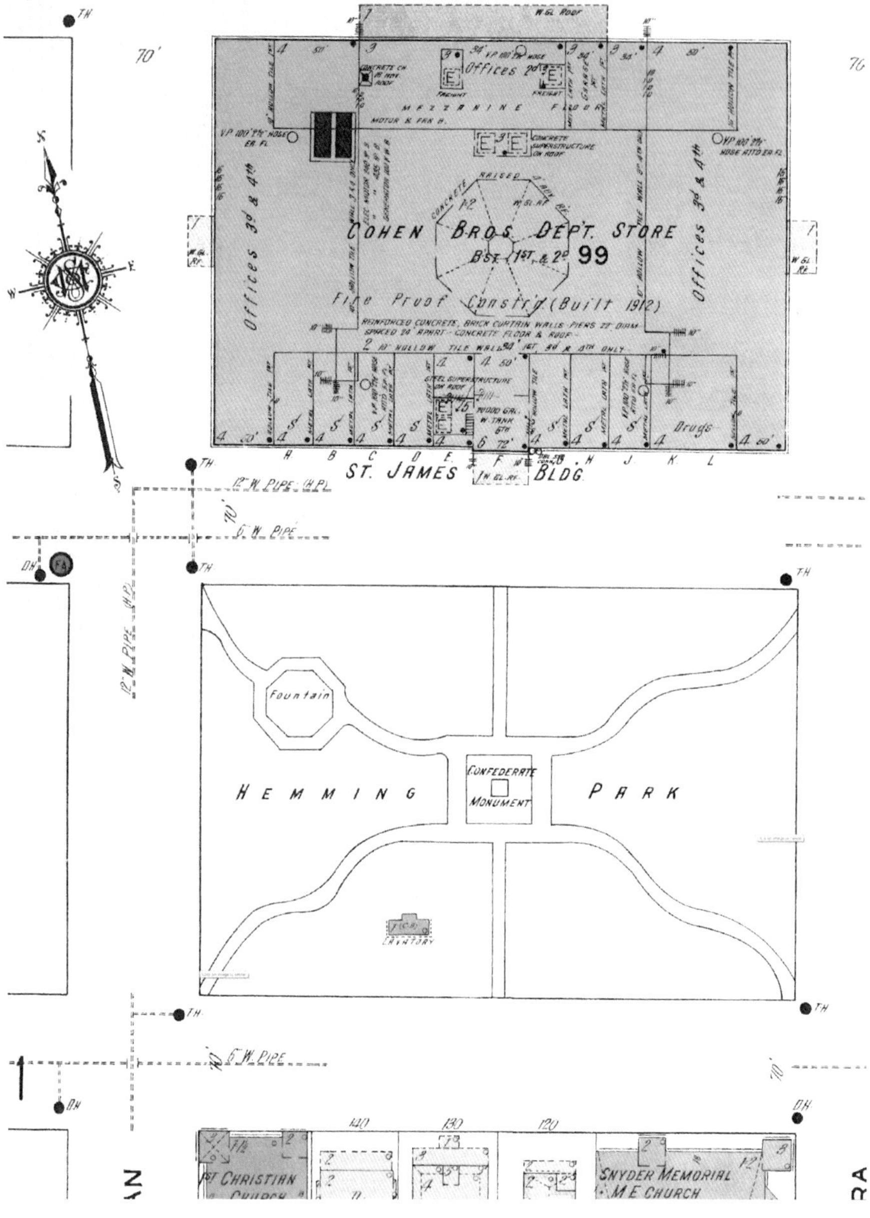

This Sanborn Fire Insurance map illustrates the general layout of the Cohen Brothers Department Store and St. James Building in 1913. *Courtesy of the University of Florida, George A. Smathers Library.*

Ortega was under construction. As the treasurer and secretary of J.N.C. Stockton's Ortega Company, Bettes selected the peninsula's Sadler's Point for his Colonial Revival home, which was designed by McClure & Holmes. Although Ortega offered acres of riverfront property, Bettes selected this inland site to avoid wind generated by the river.

While Cohen Brothers Big Store occupied the remaining portion of the first floor and the entire second floor, several companies leased office spaces on the third and fourth floors. Companies leasing space on the third floor in 1912 included the Anti-Saloon League, Talley & Summer and American Agricultural Chemical Company's Jacksonville office. Headquartered in New York City, American Agricultural Chemical's Jacksonville branch manager was W.W. Hathaway. In the early half of the twentieth century, the company operated a phosphate works along the St. Johns River. Eventually, starting in 1938, that site would become a paper mill operated by the National Container Corporation, Owens-Illinois, Alton Box Board Company and Jefferson Smurfit before being shut down in 1998. Talley & Summer was an architectural partnership formed in 1913 by Wilbur B. "Burt" Talley and J. Ernest Summer. A prominent Springfield resident, Talley was one of the founders of the Florida Institute of Architects. He worked and resided in Jacksonville until the death of his wife, Nellie, and thirteen-year-old daughter, Sarah, who were riding in a car hit by an Atlantic Coast Line passenger train on December 21, 1919. After the tragic accident, Talley relocated to Lakeland, Florida.

Also located on the third floor in room 302 was the Anti-Saloon League, the leading organization lobbying for prohibition in the country during the Progressive era. It had become a national organization in 1895, quickly rising to become the most powerful prohibition lobby in America, surpassing the Woman's Christian Temperance Union and Prohibition Party in the process. The league's most influential leaders were Wayne Wheeler, Ernest Cherrington and William "Pussyfoot" Johnson. Known for using pressure politics against "wet" candidates, the league's success led to the passage of the Eighteenth Amendment, causing breweries such as the Jax Brewing Company to lay off thousands of workers nationwide.

The fourth floor of the St. James Building was initially home to a tenant list that included H.J. Klutho's architectural practice, Western Union Telegraph Company and Phillips-Turnbull Company. Phillips-Turnbull was an engineering and contracting firm that specialized in reinforced concrete construction and real estate development. The firm's president was Frederick Phillips, and Byron E. Turnbull served as the vice-president.

During World War I, Cohen Brothers briefly operated a branch store south of Jacksonville at Camp Joseph E. Johnston. Camp Johnston occupied the site of a Florida National Guard base dating back to June 8, 1909, on the present-day site of Naval Air Station (NAS) Jacksonville, before being taken over by the federal government in September 1917. The former base had been the home of the second-largest rifle range in the country, only behind Camp Perry in Ohio. The camp, named after a Confederate general who served as the head quartermaster for the U.S. Army before the Civil War, functioned as a training center for quartermasters. These were officers whose duty was to provide other military personnel with food, shelter, clothing, fuel, stationery, storage and transportation.

By 1918, Camp Johnston had become a town of its own with twenty-seven thousand men stationed on base before leaving America for the trenches of France. Now linked to Jacksonville via an electric streetcar line, Camp Johnston contained more than six hundred buildings built in less than four months. There was a Hostess House where soldiers could meet female volunteers from town. In addition to the Cohen Brothers' branch store, the camp included a YMCA, library, canteen, motion picture theater, post office, bowling alley and billiard parlor. It was said that the doughboys of Camp Johnston loved to sing and even had some of the famous songwriters of the era, such as Abe Alman, training at the camp. Alman wrote such favorites as "Oh Johnny, Oh Johnny," "Sweetheart of Mine" and "Down Beneath the Sheltering Palms." While stationed at Camp Johnston, his new compositions included "Pick a Little Four-Leaf Clover and Send It Over to Me," "Faugh-a-Baliah" and "The Meaning of the YMCA." In mid-1918, Congress passed a $1,760,000 appropriation to expand the camp to a capacity of fifty thousand men, but the armistice of November 1918 came before work could start. By the camp's decommissioning on May 16, 1919, the branch store of Cohen Brothers had ceased operation.

By the 1920s, Charles C. Bettes' pharmacy, located on the first floor at the intersection of Laura and Duval Streets, had become known as L.K. Liggett's Drug Store. L.K. Liggett's was owned by the United Drug Company of Boston, Massachusetts, which was founded by Louis Kroh Liggett. In 1902, two decades earlier, the Detroit native and American drugstore magnate had persuaded forty independent drugstores to invest $4,000 in a retailers' cooperative called United Drug Stores, which sold products under the Rexall name. After World War I, the cooperative established a franchise arrangement whereby independently owned retail outlets adopted the Rexall trade name and sold Rexall products. The company's headquarters

The Camp Joseph E. Johnston branch of Cohens' Big Store in 1918. *Courtesy of the State Archives of Florida.*

was based in Boston, in an area now occupied by Northeastern University. Liggett's would remain a street-level fixture in the St. James Building for over three decades.

Other businesses in the mixed-use structure over the years included Armour Fertilizer Works, Florida State Marketing Bureau and the International Agricultural Corporation. The International Agricultural Corporation was incorporated in June 1909. It initially owned a number of fertilizer-manufacturing plants and large deposits of phosphate rock in Tennessee, potash mines in Germany and all of the capital stock in the Prairie Pebble Phosphate Company in Florida. It added manufacturing plants in Alabama, Georgia, Maine, New York, Pennsylvania and Tennessee within its first few years and became the largest owner and seller of phosphate rock in the United States by the mid-1920s. Its second-floor location, in room 208, served as its Jacksonville sales office and was managed by Geo V. Savita. The Florida State Marketing Bureau's printing department was also located on the second floor of the St. James Building in room 205. Created by the legislature of 1917 as a division of the State Department of Agriculture, it was one of the first departments of its kind to be established.

For several years, Armour Fertilizer Works operated its division offices out of rooms 310–13 on the third floor of the St. James Building, with Fred F. Coffee being the division manager. At the time, Armour operated fertilizer and meatpacking facilities on Talleyrand Avenue, northeast

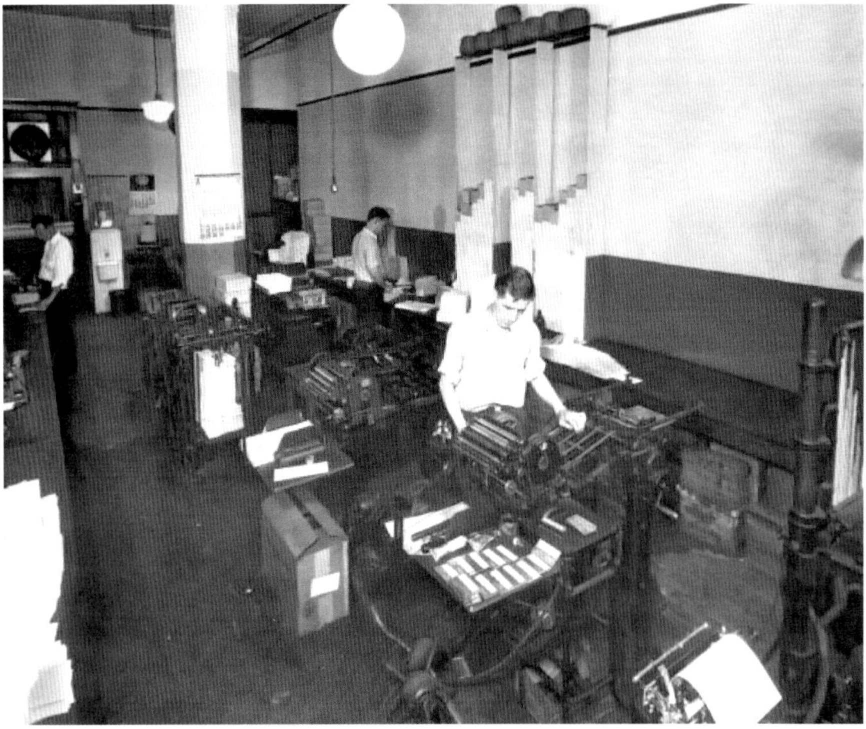

Florida State Marketing Bureau employees busy working at the print shop above Cohen Brothers' Big Store in 1937. *Courtesy of the State Archives of Florida.*

of downtown Jacksonville. Armour & Company was a slaughterhouse and meatpacking company founded in Chicago, Illinois, in 1867 by the Armour brothers. By 1880, the company was Chicago's most important business and helped make the city and its Union Stock Yards the center of the American meatpacking industry.

In the midst of a cattle shortage, Florida jumped on Armour's radar in 1912 when the company was offered five thousand heads of grass cattle in Kissimmee. After purchasing the cattle and shipping it to St. Louis, Armour sent representatives to scout the area and found prospects for beef production so good that they considered locating a plant in the state. Once this became known, prominent businessmen of Jacksonville reached out and urged Armour to erect a plant at Jacksonville. To ensure a regular supply of livestock for the plant, Armour established Interstate Stockyards near the Talleyrand slaughterhouse in 1916. By 1919, the Armour-owned Jacksonville plant was the only meatpacking plant constructed by the "Big Five" in the southeastern United States. At the time, the Big Five were Omaha's Cudahy Meatpacking and Chicago-based Armour, Swift & Company, Morris & Company and Wilson & Company.

Armour also had the largest private refrigerator car fleet in America. In 1919, the Federal Trade Commission ordered the company's sale for antitrust reasons. That entity became known as Fruit Growers Express (FGE), with its major repair shops at Jacksonville and Alexandria, Virignia. The Fruit Growers Express office was also located on the third floor of the St. James Building in room 356.

Cohen Brothers was known for its treatment of employees like family. Annual outings for store employees were commonly held at Atlantic Beach, Pablo Beach and nearby picnic grounds. The gratitude of the employees was illustrated in them presenting Jacob Cohen with a Silver Loving Cup on Christmas 1923. In addition, the Cohens routinely sponsored local baseball, bowling and basketball teams. In 1932, the Pirates, the women's basketball team, played in the WAAU National Championship Tournament and were awarded the Sportsmanship trophy.

The Big Store's popularity would result in dramatic changes to the St. James Building's architectural integrity. Sales at the department store were so good that an extra floor of retail space was desired by Cohen Brothers. In an effort to preserve the skylight court, Klutho suggested adding a fifth floor to the building. At the same time, the Cohens commissioned E.R. Beheles & Company, a Nashville, Tennessee–based architectural firm, to develop an alternative solution to meet their space demands. The E.R. Beheles plan called for the complete demolition of the skylight and its chandelier. After evaluating their options, the E.R. Beheles concept was selected above Klutho's suggestions. Disgusted with the outcome, Klutho moved his offices from the St. James Building to Springfield in 1928, with the goal of being as far from downtown as he could reasonably move.

On July 29, 1927, after an illness of several months, Jacob Elias Cohen died at his home from heart trouble and complications at the age of sixty-five. During his role as the president of Cohen Brothers, Jacob Cohen had grown to become one of Jacksonville's most progressive leaders, business-wise, civically and religiously. At the time of his death, Jacob Cohen was a valued member of the Jacksonville Chamber of Commerce and had served roles as the director of the Children's Home Society and Florida State Fair Association. In addition, he held memberships in the Lakeside, Riverside and Norwood clubs. As a sign of respect for the philanthropist, many businesses across the city closed their doors for his funeral. After the funeral, his remains

A St. James Realty and Department Store Company authorized capital stock certificate signed by Jacob Elias Cohen on September 9, 1926. *Courtesy of Whitewaycorner.com.*

were interred in the Temple Cemetery at the Cohen Mausoleum, just north of Jacksonville's Brentwood neighborhood. On October 18, 1928, a plaque in honor of Jacob Elias Cohen was installed and unveiled at the Big Store:

To perpetuate the memory of
Jacob Elias Cohen
1862–1927
Founder and President
Of
Cohen Brothers
This tablet has been erected by the executives and employees
of the state who worked with him,
who knew him and loved him.

Always interested in following the management details of her husband's department store, Jacob Cohen's widow, Hattie Halle Cohen, became the Big Store's president and chief executive. Their son, Halle, became the vice-president of the department store after the death of his father. Hattie was one of six daughters born to Philip and Minna Halle after they migrated to

Jacksonville in 1866. Three girls (Edna, Rae and Minna) and one boy (Halle) were born to Jacob and Hattie Cohen during the course of their thirty-nine-year marriage.

After the Great Fire of 1901, Jacob and Hattie raised their children in a residence at 604 North Laura Street. Located near the intersection of Laura and Ashley Streets, this site is now occupied by First Baptist Church. During the early twentieth century, Aaron and Teresa Zacharias were nearby neighbors, residing at 1006 North Laura Street, which is presently the campus of Florida State College at Jacksonville. On November 24, 1921, the Cohens' daughter Rae married the Zachariases' son Percy. When Halle Cohen eventually became the president of the Big Store, Percy Washington Zacharias served as vice-president. The Zacharias family played a critical role in the outcome of World War II. Serving in both world wars, Percy's younger brother, Ellis Mark Zacharias Sr., was a rear admiral and naval attaché to Japan. By World War II, he had become one of America's foremost intelligence experts. In spring 1945, Captain Zacharias recorded broadcasts to Tokyo as part of President Truman's call for Japan to surrender: "Your future lies in your own hands. You can choose between a wasteful, unclean death for men of your forces, or a peace with honor." After World War II, he was appointed as the deputy director of U.S. Naval Intelligence, and after retirement, he narrated the NBC television docudrama *Behind Closed Doors*.

Born in Jacksonville in 1905, Jerrold Reinarch Zacharias was the only son of Percy's older brother, Isadore Auguste Zacharias. After gaining his doctorate degree from Columbia University in 1932, he went to the Massachusetts Institute of Technology to head the Radiation Laboratory's division on radar transmitter components in 1940. After this, he went to Los Alamos, New Mexico, to serve as the director of the engineering division of the Manhattan Project. The Manhattan Project was a research and development program led by the United States with participation from the United Kingdom and Canada that produced the first atomic bomb during World War II.

The Cohens' daughter Minna married Robert Lewis Seitner Jr. on October 1, 1921. With Halle Cohen and Percy Zacharias, Seitner assisted Hattie Cohen in running the store's operations. While serving as company president, Hattie continued to promote the charitable policies of her husband.

The Big Store was also well known for its alluring and spirited window displays. For decades, the changing displays mesmerized shoppers. For example, in November 1915, the Cohen displays hosted the World's Rarest Shoe Collection, which featured a sixteenth-century Hungarian cavalry boot

The Big Store's window displays were known for drawing large crowds. *Courtesy of Drew Kaplan.*

and a velvet shoe from Turkey. This traveling display had been coordinated by R.R. Wilkinson, a shoe buyer for the Big Store, who encountered it on a buying trip to San Francisco. At the time, it was being viewed by millions at the 1915 Panama-Pacific Exposition.

In 1928, Cohen Brothers retained Edna Kirby to come to Jacksonville. Kirby was a famed actress with Paramount who was known as the "Girl Who Lives in Glass Houses." That March, she "lived" in the Big Store's display windows for a full week, eating, sleeping, entertaining and modeling clothes while thousands of Jaxsons looked on at the four display windows at the intersection of Laura and Duval Streets. The Cohens went as far as to install microphones so the window watchers could listen to the movie star. Miss Kirby's stay ended on a Saturday night with her getting married in the Cohen Brothers window display. She moved out for her honeymoon.

During the 1930s, the Big Store became a sponsor of WMBR radio. WMBR was established as a one-hundred-watt AM station by F.J. Reynolds,

Inc. in June 1927. In January 1934, Reynolds relocated WMBR to Jacksonville from Tampa, setting up offices and studios atop the thirteen-story Carling Hotel on West Adams Street. In early 1949, WTVJ–Channel 4 in Miami became Florida's first television station. Less than six months later, on September 15, 1949, WMBR radio launched WMBR-TV, becoming the second television station in Florida. WMBR-TV was a CBS affiliate and, for several years, was the only CBS station between Savannah, Georgia, and Orlando, Florida. In 1953, the Washington Post Company acquired the stations. Washington Post sold WMBR radio in 1958, and the television station was rebranded as WJXT TV-4.

After seven years of serving as the Big Store's president, Hattie Halle Cohen passed away on April 13, 1935, at the age of sixty-eight. She was interred at the Cohen Mausoleum at the Temple Cemetery plot located within Evergreen Cemetery. After her death, son Halle Cohen became the president and chairman of the board of the store, which employed 450 workers in 1936. A member of the board of trustees of the Temple Ahavath Chesed, Halle was known for being a compassionate, generous and modest individual. According to Beatruce Peiser's 1936 "Pioneers of the South" article in the *Southern Israelite*, there was no temple activity that did not have

The Jacksonville Fire Department at Hemming Park during the 1920s. *Courtesy of Whitewaycorner.com.*

his active support. It further stated that Halle's greatest joy occurred in being able to "think up" something new to do for the welfare of the congregation. A true man of the community, Halle felt the same way about the department store that his father and uncles had established. Halle was routinely featured in the Cohen Brothers *Big Store News* publication. In the November 1940 edition, he wrote, "No man liveth to himself and no man dieth to himself. I want to do something while I live on this earth. I do the best I can. I'll keep on doing it. If the end comes out all right, that's all right. Nothing said against me will make any difference. Every man has his faults—you see his and he sees yours."

Like his father, Halle was a philanthropist who did many things without the need for public fanfare. He founded the Jacksonville Safety Council and was a 32nd Degree Mason who played the drums for the Shrine band. He also headed every March of Dimes campaign as long as President Franklin D. Roosevelt was alive. In addition, in 1954, the noted horticulturalist founded the Jacksonville Rose Society, which still exists today. Also a horticulturalist, Halle's wife, Nellie McArthur Cohen, was elected president of the Garden Club of Jacksonville in the spring of 1945. After her term expired in 1947, she continued as the club's building chairman. In 1951, she was the president of the Florida Federation of Garden Clubs, becoming the third Jacksonville member to serve as a state president. The other two were Merle B. Mann and Ninah May Holden Cummer. Ninah Cummer, the wife of Arthur G. Cummer, organized the club in her home on March 25, 1922, and was the first president. When it came to horticulture, Mr. and Mrs. Cohen worked as a team. The extensive gardens at their home on River Road were always open to visitors, and the Cohens were instrumental in organizing the Men's Garden Club and lobbying efforts for the selection of the Sabal palmetto as the state tree.

Throughout the Great Depression and World War II, Jacksonville continued to grow at a rapid pace, increasing in population from 129,549 in 1930 to 173,065 in 1940. In 1941, to better accommodate the Big Store's rapidly increasing popularity and customer base, Halle Cohen established a warehouse for the department store, thirteen blocks west of Hemming Plaza at 1242 West Church Street. Located in the community of LaVilla, at the intersection of West Church and Edith Streets, the two-story brick warehouse complex dated back to 1921, when it was constructed by Walter J. Bryson for the Bryson Live Stock Company. Walter Bryson and his wife, Alice, were Springfield residents who resided at 403 West Ninth Street. Prior to its acquisition by Cohen Brothers, the 27,922-square-foot space had been briefly occupied by L&L Freight Lines. In 1960, an additional 15,968 square

Marjorie Kinnan Rawlings with Robert Camp at an autographing party for Cross Creek & Cross Creek Cookery at Cohens department store in Jacksonville in 1942. *Courtesy of the Marjorie Kinnan Rawlings Collection, Special Collections and Area Studies Department, University of Florida.*

feet was added. With an additional 43,890 square feet at their disposal, the Church Street warehouses were utilized for the storage of appliances and furniture through 1968 before being replaced by a warehouse facility on Jacksonville's Westside.

By the end of World War II, the Big Store had been in business for thirty-three years. To accommodate the changes in technology, shopping trends and market demographics, the time had come to renovate and modernize the Big Store. The store's $2.5 million renovation and modernization program would be handled by Amos Parrish and Company of New York. At the time, Amos Parrish was a well-known department store consulting firm. Locally, Kenyon Drake and Associates was commissioned as the architectural firm in charge and S.S. Jacobs hired as the project's general contractor. Architectural plans included the installation of escalators and the removal of the building's third-floor octagonal glass dome. This allowed the open area in the center of

Constructed in 1921 for the Bryson Live Stock Company, this West Church Street warehouse in the neighborhood of LaVilla was utilized by Cohen Brothers between 1941 and 1968 for the storage of appliances and furniture. *Courtesy of the author.*

the U-shaped fourth floor to be filled in for additional leasable office space for the St. James Realty and Department Store Company. This modification created space for the third floor of the building to be devoted to a furniture department for the Big Store, which was originally only two floors when it opened in 1912.

On Monday, July 18, 1949, thousands of guests attended the grand opening of the Big Store's new 62,500-square-foot third floor. According to Cohen Brothers executives, the new floor was built for beauty as well as for budgets. The new floor was not only a decorator's dream come true but was also a model of efficiency that would enable the Big Store to pass on unusual operational savings to its customers.

A unique feature of the furniture department was its series of model display rooms, showing furniture as it would look in customers' homes, complete with correlated drapes, pictures, lamps and other accessories. "All our designing has had one objective—to place the greatest unobtrusive setting where the greatest number of customers can visualize how what

The addition of a third and fourth floor to the center of the St. James Building over the years can be clearly seen in this view of the Church Street elevation. *Courtesy of the author.*

they want will look in their own home," said Charles J. Breyer, executive designer for Amos Parrish and Company. In addition, the new floor featured a modern decorating studio staffed with trained decorating consultants to assist customers on product groupings, colors and periods.

With the major renovation and expansion project complete, the Big Store's workforce had increased to over nine hundred employees. To accommodate this growth in employment, a cafeteria, an employees' lounge and an eight-bed hospital had also been added to the department store.

One of the Big Store's most famed employees was Archie Eason. Eason started working with Cohens during the late 1940s as a stockman while living in Jacksonville's Miramar neighborhood at 4635 Redwood Avenue. According to Easton, he was a stock boy with a flair for ribbons who fooled around in the Big Store's hat department long enough to develop into a milliner sans pareil at Cohen Brothers through the 1950s. Around 1959, Eason left Jacksonville for the New York millinery couture, where his creations became a must for the fashionably aware woman. With the back of each hat trademarked by a green

A Cohen Brothers advertisement in the 1951–59 Temple Ahavath Chesed Yearbook. *Courtesy of the Temple Congregation Ahavath Chesed.*

A cover of the Cohen Brothers Book Department *Bookshop News* August 1951 reading guide. *Courtesy of Ron Chamblin and Chamblin's Uptown.*

sequin, his hats were worn by celebrities throughout the 1960s and 1970s. Eason's hat designs were so expensive that women were known to sew his signature green sequin onto lesser styles. During his career, he started a fashion craze with Faye Dunaway's crepe beret and designed several headdresses for Miss America pageants.

After spending three weeks in a local hospital suffering from a long illness, Halle Cohen died at 8:30 p.m. on March 10, 1956. Funeral services were held on March 12, 1956. In respect for its president and the Cohen family, the department store closed all day the Monday after Halle's death. On March 21, 1956, Colonel Robert Lewis Seitner, the brother-in-law of Halle Cohen, became the president of Cohen Brothers.

Chapter 5

A New Name

On November 24, 1958, after announcing intentions of expanding to Jacksonville in June 1958, St. Louis–based May Department Stores acquired the Cohen Brothers Department Store by signing a thirty-year lease agreement with the Jacksonville landmark. The purchase officially made Cohens the forty-seventh store in the May chain. Of interesting note, May's founder, David May, financially assisted and advised Jacob Cohen with the development of downtown Jacksonville's Big Store in 1912.

May established the May Department Stores Company in 1877. His canvas-roofed makeshift shop opened in the then populous city of Leadville, Colorado, during a gold strike. A year earlier, prospectors had discovered several silver lead deposits in the area, leading to the founding of Leadville in 1877 and setting off the Colorado silver boom. By 1880, Leadville was one of the world's largest silver camps and Colorado's second most populous city after Denver with forty thousand residents. Around 1883, outlaw Doc Holliday moved to Leadville shortly after his gunfight at the O.K. Corral. A year later, on August 19, 1884, Holliday shot ex–Leadville policeman Billy Allen after Allen threatened Holliday for failing to pay a five-dollar debt. Despite overwhelming evidence implicating him, a jury found Holliday not guilty of the shooting or attempted murder.

Despite Leadville's rapid surge as a booming silver mining town, David May came to the conclusion that there was no future in Leadville and moved his family to Denver in 1889 before settling in St. Louis in 1893.

There, he opened the Famous Clothing Store. In 1911, May merged his Famous Clothing Store with the William Barr Dry Goods Company to form Famous-Barr. His company's next expansion was the acquisition of Los Angeles–based A. Hamburger & Sons Company in 1923. Upon this acquisition, the store was renamed May Company California. In 1946, May acquired Pittsburgh-based Kaufmann's but retained it as a separate division. A year later, May acquired Strouss-Hirshberg Company of Youngstown, Ohio. In 1938, May became the first department store chain to expand with a full line store in the suburbs with the opening of a branch in Los Angeles. In 1956, May returned to Denver with the acquisition of the Daniels & Fisher Company, which was renamed May D&F division and included a massive 420,000-square-foot store in downtown Denver. By the 1957 fiscal year, the May Company's annual sales had eclipsed $533 million when it was announced that it would merge with the Hecht Company, which had sales of $105 million itself. In addition, the company unveiled its plan to finance the construction of new suburban shopping centers and department stores throughout the country, intending to spend nearly $60 million implementing this strategy by 1962.

By this time, the May Company was under the direction of Morton David May, the grandson of company founder David May. The younger May attended Dartmouth College before graduating in 1936 and entering the military as a lieutenant junior grade in the United States Naval Reserve. During World War II, he won two battle stars and the Presidential Unit Citation for service in the South Pacific. Before replacing his father, Morton Jay May, as company president in 1951, May spent two years in Jacksonville on the staff of the admiral in command of Naval Air Operational Training Command at the Jacksonville Naval Air Station.

Under the direction of Morton D. May and plans for continued expansion, the May Company turned its sights on Jacksonville's Cohen Brothers Department Store. The company's determination to make Cohen Brothers its first store in the southeastern United States came as a result of a study detailing dramatic growth in the Jacksonville region. After three months of extensive negotiations between Colonel Robert Lewis Seitner and Morton D. May, a lease agreement was made on November 24, 1958, which gave May Department Stores Company the management of Cohen Brothers. At the time, Seitner was the president of the St. James Realty and Department Store Company, which was the owner of Cohen Brothers. Upon signing the lease, May stated that nothing had made him happier than to bring Cohen Brothers into the

Cohens display counters showing "Florida fashions" in 1935. *Courtesy of the Jacksonville Historical Society.*

May chain as its forty-seventh store: "I love Jacksonville—I was stationed at the Naval Air Station here for two years during World War II and now I'll have a good reason to visit here frequently."

The lease was for a thirty-year period, with options for two renewals for fifteen years each. In addition to the long-term lease of the store property, the May Company purchased all of Cohen Brothers' liquid assets, including its stock of merchandise, accounts receivable, furniture and fixtures. According to Morton May, "We are not running a race to operate the largest retail company in this country but with today's purchase we may well be doing just that."

Despite having forty-seven stores and being known as the world's largest full-line department store chain, May saw itself as a "family of stores" instead of a chain. To maintain the brand that Cohen Brothers had established after being in business for ninety-one years, the store was renamed May-Cohens. May said:

> *We are a family of stores. Each store is autonomous, operated by its own management and staff who are expected to become members of the community and play an important civic role in it. That's exactly what we intend to do here.*
>
> *Cohen Brothers is one of the South's outstanding stores now. We intend to keep it just that. We will continue to maintain an excellent and varied stock of merchandise, and price-wise we will meet our competition head-on, even the discount houses.*

With its buying power and experience, the May Company believed it could improve the Big Store both in service to the customer and from a merchandising standpoint.

As part of the transition, Ralph E. Doughton was named the first president and general manager of the new department store division. Prior to May-Cohens, Doughton—a Birmingham, Alabama native with thirty years of retailing experience—was a member of the executive staff of Famous-Barr, the May Company's St. Louis–based store. In addition, former Cohen Brothers president Colonel Robert Lewis Seitner remained with the store as the chairman of the board of the new operating company. D.H. Stynchcomb remained as the executive vice-president and assistant general manager and James E. McGregor as general merchandising manager and member of the board.

Major expansion and change in the Jacksonville market would come with May's acquisition of Cohen Brothers. Upon his first visit to Jacksonville, chairman of the board and former company president Morton Jay May announced major changes were in store for the Big Store. May had hired Ketchum and Sharp, a New York–based architectural firm, to plan the face-lifting and renovation of the downtown Jacksonville store, which was recognized as a Prairie School masterpiece.

After three months of surveying the facilities, Ralph Doughton announced intentions for extensive renovation of the store's basement and first floor. With no initial desire to alter the building's exterior, the company's $2 million renovation plans included installing an escalator to the basement, the expansion of the first floor's mezzanine level and two new street-level entrances. However, by the end of the renovation project, the building's first-floor storefronts were modernized as well.

Changes in the basement involved a complete renovation, which effectively doubled the size of its retail floor area. Designed to be a store within itself, basement improvements featured new escalators and an enlarged housewares section. The first floor received new fixtures throughout, with the regrouping and relocation of most of the departments on this level. Ceiling heights were dropped with the intention of creating the effect of a brand-new store. In addition, the first-floor restaurant was enlarged and the mezzanine level, where linens were located, was expanded by 50 percent. Changes on the second floor included rearrangement and expansion of the children's department and the addition of a three-hundred-seat auditorium intended to serve both the store and community. On the third floor, several departments were relocated to other floors to create five thousand square feet of additional space for the furniture department. The fourth floor, which was used for storing and receiving stock, was rearranged for greater internal efficiency. The targeted completion date for the major renovation project was the fall of 1960.

Other departments in the rebranded Big Store included the shoe department, which was located in the basement level, which was also known as the May-Cohens Budget Floor. Street-level departments included drugs, jewelry, the beauty salon, handbags, Florida Shop and the Price Candy Company. The second floor's sections included women's apparel and a photographic studio, while the third floor included a fabric center and records shop. The fourth floor of the building housed the Big Store's candy kitchen, along with a large number of smaller businesses, most of which were dentists and physicians.

Many residents remembered the Big Store's candy department for its chocolate-covered miracles, known as Annaclairs, and its Strawberries in the Snow. The fourth-floor candy kitchen was operated by the Price Candy Company. For several decades, the Big Store allowed school groups to take tours of the production facility. The Price Candy Company had a tremendous reputation throughout the country for crafting quality chocolates. It was established in 1913 by Charles Price at the confectionery department of the Jones Store Company in downtown Kansas City, Missouri. By the late 1940s, Price—along with Russell Stover Candies, Sunshine Biscuit Company, Sifers Confection Company, Dye Candy Company, Hill Candy Company, Missouri Candy Company and the Crane Chocolate Company—had transformed the candy-making business into Kansas City's fourth-largest industry. In May 2000, with the shutdown of its Richmond, Missouri factory, the confectionery manufacturer closed for good after eighty-seven years of operation.

The Annaclair was Price's most recognized product. Named for Charles Price's two favorite dippers, Anna and Clair, the candy was known for having a rich, creamy vanilla center, coated in milk or dark chocolate and chopped

A 1960s May-Cohens newspaper advertisement. *Courtesy of the Jacksonville Public Library Special Collections Department.*

pecans. Alex Phillips worked in Price's candy factory on the fourth floor of the Big Store for thirty-four years. Known as the "Candy Man," Phillips joined Cohen Brothers at the age of twenty-one as a busboy in the Big Store's first-floor restaurant. He eventually became a stockman and a candy maker's helper before being taken into the department's inner circle of candy making. According to Phillips in a 1979 *Florida Times-Union* interview, "They didn't want their secrets out."

Other treats produced in the candy department included peanut brittle, cashew brittle, Strawberries in the Snow and Turks. Turks were pecans covered with caramel and chocolate. Strawberries in the Snow were candies produced by dipping individual strawberries into white chocolate. When made available to shoppers, the chocolate-covered strawberries routinely sold out in a few hours. Looking back on his career, Phillips enjoyed his time in the Big Store's candy factory: "It never was boring. I enjoyed it. I got a lot of pleasure out of it. I got a lot of calories, too!"

Over the years, operating individual candy-making operations in department stores became inefficient for the Price Candy Company. According to Dave Mastricola of Price Candy Company in 1979, "The smaller factories weren't being able to produce at a cost that we could afford to keep them open. We had a large plant in Kansas City, so we decided it would be cheaper to make all the candy there." The Price Candy Company ceased the Big Store's candy production facility in 1976, converting the space into a storage operation for candies shipped to Jacksonville from its Midwest factory.

The same day the May Company inked the lease for the acquisition of Cohen Brothers, May announced plans for the construction of a seven-level parking garage as part of a joint venture with Robert H. Jacobs, president of Jacksonville-based S.S. Jacobs Company. The site of this project consisted of two large surface parking lots opposite the department store at the intersection of Laura and Church Streets. The 200,000-square-foot, five-hundred-space parking garage was estimated to cost $1.5 million to construct and would be built on land obtained under a sixty-five-year lease from the Alcliff Investment Company and T.T. and E.L. Phillips Jr. The garage would be designed by George A. Devlin, president of National Garages, which was known as one of the top multi-level parking garage designers at the time.

Before the day was over, May and Jacobs also stated that they were contemplating the erection of a twenty- to thirty-story office building at the northeast corner of Laura and Church Streets. By March 14, 1959, the joint venture between the May Company and S.S. Jacobs Company became

Shoppers swarm the first floor of the Big Store to test out the new escalators. *Courtesy of the Jacksonville Historical Society.*

known as Downtown Center. Ketchum & Sharp, the New York firm hired to redesign the former Cohen Brothers Big Store, was retained to design the $15 million mixed-use development, which was anchored by two major retailers that complemented May-Cohens, realizing the dream of Jacob Cohen in 1912, fifty years earlier, when he envisioned his new Big Store being the catalyst for major development on the surrounding blocks.

The parking garage announced the same day the May Company agreed to acquire Cohens was the first phase of Downtown Center to be completed, opening on November 13, 1960, and featuring a new twenty-five-thousand-square-foot location for Purcell's Women's Store at ground level. Purcell's offered fine clothing, from gloves and lingerie to shoes and hats, while coining itself as "the specialty shop of individuality." "The new store will give us more than double the space we now have and the move is in keeping with the natural growth direction of Downtown and a mounting trend for modern stores to become part of a planned center with parking, offices, a restaurant, recreational facilities and professional offices in proximity," said Richard J. Lewinson, Purcell's president and general manager.

That same year, several cultural events occurred, solidifying the Big Store's Hemming Park location as the epicenter of Jacksonville. In August 1960, the Big Store was thrust into the forefront of the civil rights demonstrations by the NAACP Youth Council focused on bringing down the barriers of segregation at downtown department stores. Although the youth council intended to target the Big Store's restaurant and the lunch counters at five and dime stores W.T. Grant, Kress and McCrory's, its members decided that their first sit-in would take place on Saturday, August 13, 1960, at F.W. Woolworth because of its strategic location.

Two weeks later, on August 27, 1960, forty NAACP Youth Council demonstrators peacefully sat in at W.T. Grant's Department Store on the corner of Adams and Main Streets. A second group headed for the lunch counters at F.W. Woolworth's, which, like the Big Store, overlooked Hemming Park. Alton Yates, then a twenty-one-year-old member of the youth council, recalled, "We saw a large number of trucks parked at Hemming Plaza. There were white men on the back of those trucks handing out ax handles and baseball bats to other men." Rodney Hurst, then a sixteen-year-old

Overlooking Hemming Plaza and the Big Store, the F.W. Woolworth lunch counter was the site of an NAACP Youth Council demonstration culminating in what has become known as Ax Handle Saturday on August 27, 1960. *Courtesy of the State Archives of Florida.*

freshman at Edward Waters College, added, "We were met by more than 200 whites with ax handles. All of us got hit. You saw everything in a blur." To protect the students, a number of youth from the Sugar Hill neighborhood's Wilder Park, the Boomerangs, swooped in to serve as a buffer between the students and the mob. At the end of the day, sixty-two people were arrested, and the aftermath made history all over the country. Now known as Ax Handle Saturday, the event symbolized a wake-up call in Jacksonville's civil rights movement and became the turning point for a city evolving from a segregated community to a place of equality and dignity for all citizens.

On October 18, 1960, presidential candidates Vice President Richard Nixon and Senator John F. Kennedy spoke at the park the Big Store overlooked. The event attracted crowds that were said to be the largest in the history of the park. In addition, Robert Kennedy, Senator Barry Goldwater, Rose Kennedy and Senator Lyndon Johnson also campaigned in the area that month. Goldwater's speech at Hemming Park drew a crowd of over one thousand.

In 1962, Purcell's former Hemming Park location a block south at 305 North Laura Street became the home of the Luggage Shop, a downtown

Vice presidential candidate Lyndon Johnson speaking to Jacksonville residents in front of the Big Store in Hemming Park in 1960. *Courtesy of the State Archives of Florida.*

retailer that dated back to 1919. That same year, the new Purcell's store was joined by J.B. Ivey & Company's six-story, 180,000-square-foot department store at the northeast corner of Laura and Church Streets. J.B. Ivey & Company was a Charlotte, North Carolina–based department store chain founded by Joseph Benjamin Ivey in 1900. The downtown Jacksonville store, which opened in August 1962, was the chain's seventh and the first major department store to be constructed in a metropolitan United States downtown location in thirty years. According to Ivey's president, George Ivey, "We have long known that Jacksonville is a city in which we would like to establish a store in the downtown area." Anticipating future growth, the department store's foundation was designed for the building to be able to accommodate two additional floors as needed.

The Jewelry, Shoe Salon, Men's Furnishing, Men's University Shop and Plaza Sportswear sections were some of the departments located on the building's first floor. Departments located on the second floor included

The shadow of the St. James Building dominates this 2012 view of the former J.B. Ivey's & Company department store. When the six-level store opened in 1962, it was said to be the first major department store to be constructed in a metropolitan United States downtown location in thirty years. *Courtesy of the author.*

Moderate Dresses, Juniors and Coats, while the third floor featured Lingerie, Children's Clothing and Sportswear. Also, Brother's Restaurant was located on the third floor of the new Ivey's store. The Furniture, Carpet and Draperies departments were located on the fourth floor. Home Entertainment, China and Linens occupied the fifth floor. In addition to billing itself as "Jacksonville's most beautiful department store," the store also offered free parking for the first two hours in the garage under the building.

The $12 million Universal Marion Building was the crown jewel of Downtown Center when it opened its doors in 1963. At the time, the 268-foot-tall, nineteen-story tower was the tallest building on the Northbank and second tallest in the city. The building housed the Internal Revenue Service and law and insurance offices. The Universal Marion Company was the largest tenant. Founded by Louis Elwood Wolfson—a Wall Street financier and eventually the owner of the 1978 American Triple Crown winner Affirmed—Universal Marion owned the *Miami Beach Sun* and *Jacksonville Chronicle* newspapers and made movies through a subsidiary. The firm co-financed the production of Mel Brooks' first movie, *The Producers*, which won an Oscar and later became a major Broadway play. It also funded Woody Allen's first movie, *Take the Money and Run*. In 1946, Louis Wolfson's family foundation donated $500,000 to create the Wolfson Children's Hospital, and Wolfson High School is named for Louis' brother Samuel. The family also donated to Jacksonville University and funded construction of Wolfson Park, the minor-league baseball park in Jacksonville for decades. A millionaire by the age of twenty-eight, Wolfson became a nationally known figure when he unsuccessfully attempted a hostile takeover of Montgomery Ward and Company in 1955.

The Embers, a 250-seat restaurant, opened on the eighteenth floor of the Universal Marion building in 1964. At the Embers, live Maine lobsters were flown in from Booth Bay, Maine, every Friday at the restaurant, which stayed open until 12:30 a.m. daily. Rotating 360 degrees every one and a half hours, it was said to be the largest revolving restaurant in the world.

Chapter 6

Growing Up Around the Big Store

The May Company's acquisition of Cohen Brothers and joint venture with S.S. Jacobs Company, which resulted in J.B. Ivey's opening next door, was the culmination of an urban landscape envisioned by Jacob Cohen in 1912. Over the course of forty-eight years, the Big Store had successfully become the anchor of a downtown retail environment featuring several major department stores within a five-block radius of Hemming Park. Over the years, each store earned its place within Jacksonville's economic and social structure. As many as six major retailers, including the Big Store, had clustered along Hogan Street between Hemming Park and the St. Johns River. Three were located at the intersection of Hogan and Adams Streets. Prior to 1936, Hogan Street had developed as one of the Jacksonville Traction Company's major north–south corridors for its sixty-mile streetcar network.

Levy's Department Store

The pattern of establishing Hogan Street as Jacksonville's department store central had begun with Jacob Cohen's decision to construct the St. James Building adjacent to the Windsor Hotel and Hemming Park after the Great Fire of 1901. This pattern received a significant boost from rapid population growth throughout Jacksonville and Florida leading up to the Great Depression. Between 1900 and 1930, the city underwent a period of

Benjamin Levy's elaborately designed Levy's Department Store building opened on the northeast corner of Hogan and Adams Streets in 1927, becoming the first department store to follow the Big Store's decision to relocate from Bay Street to the vicinity of Hemming Park. *Courtesy of the City of Jacksonville Historic Preservation Office.*

unprecedented growth, increasing in population from 28,429 to 129,549. The city's streetcar network had increased from twelve miles of track in 1898 to fifty-nine miles of track in 1930. With 12,000 people passing through the railroad terminal on a daily basis, Jacksonville had become known as the "Gateway City of the South." Its economy had effectively changed from tourist based in the late nineteenth century to one in which the leading industries in 1925 were shipbuilding, lumber and cigar manufacturing. Furthermore, by the Roaring Twenties, the Big Store had become a significant anchor in the downtown retail scene, causing additional retailers—such as Bellinger's Pharmacy, C.H. Edwards Photography and Vogue Ladies Wear—to either relocate or open in the vicinity of Hemming Park. In 1927, a second major retailer migrated north in the vicinity of Hemming Park in the form of Levy's Department Store. Levy's opened at the intersection of Adams and Hogan Streets, adjacent to the Hogan Street streetcar line connecting downtown Jacksonville with Springfield.

Levy's was founded in 1912 by Benjamin S. Levy, who was residing in the Hotel Burbridge shortly after relocating to Jacksonville with his wife, Della. The original Levy's store was located just south of the Seminole Hotel in a small structure on the northeast corner of Hogan and Bay Streets. Levy's, which had a reputation for carrying some of the most exclusive and luxurious merchandise, billed itself as the store "where the styles are shown first" and the "home of Hart, Schaffner and Marx Clothes." Jacob Jewelers owner Roy Thomas remarked in a September 2010 *Jacksonville Daily Record* interview, "Levy's was a fine store. I bought all my clothes there. It was the only store in town that sold Hollywood suits. They were handstitched and cost $300 back then. They also sold Italian shoes."

With Levy serving as the company president and Walter Brownlow as the vice-president, the department store specialized in men's and women's apparel, shoes, millinery, ladies' hosiery and handbags. Levy's four-story structure was one of four large, eclectic Chicago School–style buildings constructed within three blocks of one another by Marsh & Saxelbye, a popular local architectural firm during the 1920s, during a two-year stretch between 1926 and 1927. Costing $425,000 to construct, except for the building's polished granite base, the entire structure was cladded in terra cotta, a molded and fired ceramic material that is highly decorative and moderately durable. The main entrance to Levy's was set in a Palladium bay with three arched openings with rusticated surrounds and ornamented keystones. Departments featuring jewelry, accessories and bags were located on Levy's first floor. The second floor featured shoes and a fashion salon, while the upper floors housed apparel.

Rosenblum's

In 1934, Rosenblum's opened its doors in the Akers-Cody Building at the intersection of Hogan and Adams Streets. The Akers-Cody Building had been designed by E.R. Merry Architect and constructed by Griffin Construction Company in 1921. This retailer was one of the first men's clothing stores in the city when it originally opened at Bay and Clay Streets. Rosenblum's start dated back to 1896, when founder Frank "Papa" Rosenblum started peddling pots, pans and linens from a horse-and-buggy on downtown Jacksonville's streets. Unlike most clothing merchants of the era who settled in Jacksonville, the Rosenblum family did not come from

In 1937, Rosenblum's relocated to the thirty-six-thousand-square-foot Akers-Cody Building on the southwest corner of Hogan and Adams Streets, becoming a luxury retailer that competed directly with neighboring department stores in the vicinity of Hemming Park. *Courtesy of the State Archives of Florida.*

New York. Instead, Frank Rosenblum migrated to Jacksonville from Key West. By the turn of the century, Rosenblum had opened his first store at Bay and Clay Streets. After the Great Fire of 1901, he relocated his business to 410 Main Street. In 1922, the store expanded into a larger location at 340 Main Street, near the old Duval High School. With the opening of its thirty-six-thousand-square-foot store at Adams and Hogan, Rosenblum's became a luxury retailer competing directly with neighboring department stores.

FURCHGOTT'S OF FLORIDA

With World War II underway and the Great Depression coming to an end, the 1940s ushered in major changes for the Big Store and the retail environment it anchored. The first major change was the relocation of Furchgott's Department Store to a site within two blocks of Cohen Brothers Big Store on October 8, 1941. Earmarking the site of the old United States Post Office at the intersection of Adams and Hogan Streets, adjacent to Levy's and Rosenblum's, Furchgott's new department store promised to transform the intersection into one of downtown's major retail areas. Like Cohen Brothers, Furchgott's had become a longtime Jacksonville institution. Furchgott's Inc. was established by Leopold Furchgott in 1868. During the company's early years, it was known as Kohn-Furchgott & Benedict and was located at the southwest corner of Bay and Main Streets. Like Jacob Cohen, Furchgott was considered a local visionary. His store was the first to have elevators in Jacksonville, the first to introduce home deliveries by automobile and the first to employ women on its sales staff. Under the leadership of company president Frederick Meyerheim, Furchgott's went through a period of growth that called for a major expansion of its upscale downtown department store, which was known for its designer departments. To accommodate this growth, the impressive and towering marble post office building was demolished to make way for a new sixty-thousand-square-foot, six-level Art Deco department store designed by Marsh and Saxelbye Architects.

According to Furchgott's executives, the new store was a "scientifically-designed" structure, specially created for the customers' shopping pleasure and convenience. Furchgott's basement level was the place where "prices were low and bargains universal." In addition, an attraction of the basement level was the delivery room's chute. There, packages for delivery or mail were sent from any of the five floors above down the chute and emptied into a tunnel resembling a dairy silo.

A company brochure described the department store's first floor as being as typically American as "cheese and apple pie." A diverse number of items, including tuxedos, topcoats, diamonds, silverware, costume jewelry, gloves, neckwear, lingerie, umbrellas, gifts and pens and pencils, was available.

Featuring a round room resembling a historic Queen Anne drawing room at the center, Furchgott's second floor was tailor made for the Jacksonville female. Anchoring this floor were the women's ready-to-wear, shoe, sportswear, negligee, junior clothing, fur salon and alterations departments. Furthermore, this floor housed a women's lounge and Bride's Room, where complete trousseaux could be selected in quiet seclusion. The third floor was of especial interest to Jaxons with growing families. A variety of items including children's wardrobes, toys, luggage, radios, radios and sheet music were available on this level.

Like the Big Store, Leopold Furchgott's department store was a Jacksonville retail institution that dated back to the 1860s. In 1941, Furchgott's completed construction of its five-level flagship department store on the southeast corner of Hogan and Adams Streets, going head to head with Levy's, Rosenblum's and Cohens. *Courtesy of the State Archives of Florida.*

Necessities such as bedding, rugs, lamps, linens and notions were located on the fourth floor. In addition, the northwest corner of the fourth floor was home to Furchgott's drapery department. Here, a decorator-inspired drapery showroom was used to market the latest trends in home furnishings, and expert advice was offered here. The fifth floor was originally an open court area that was enclosed four years after the opening of the store in 1945. The floor's occupants included the layaway department, an upholstery workroom and a display workroom, along with offices for credit, employment, advertising and the store's executives. Other features included a "hospital room," an employees' recreation terrace and the staff restrooms.

Furchgott's was viewed by local residents as a fancy store. According to longtime Jacksonville resident Paul Bremer:

> *They carried the best of everything. When you entered the store, the street level floor was always decorated elaborately, up to the ceilings, with the seasonal decorations. They didn't have to rely on Sunday advertising inserts to get customers. Just walking by their store on the sidewalk, you looked in their windows and saw wonderful displays of merchandise that encouraged you* [to] *go in and shop. The elevators were run by ladies who sat on a little wooden seat and told you which floor carried the items you wanted. The clerks knew their departments and were very helpful getting you just the right items. If you needed clothes, they helped you size them and try them on. Real customer service. Downtown had inexpensive merchandise stores, and then they had Cohens, Rosenblum's, and Furchgott's.*

JCPenney Company, Inc.

In 1950, the Windsor Hotel was demolished to make room for a parking lot. According to I. Morris, vice-president of the Cuyahoga Wrecking Company, the hotel had held the strangest treasure he ever found during a demolition: a subterranean room filled with illegal whiskey. In 1955, the Big Store received new neighbors in the form of F.W. Woolworth and JCPenney as replacements on the site that had once been occupied by Hotel Windsor. Both stores were located in a single structure anchoring the west side of Hemming Park at the intersection of Monroe and Hogan Streets.

F.W. Woolworth relocated from its store on Main and Forsyth and opened its 16,350-square-foot Hemming Park store in March 1955. The basement

JCPenney's ninety-thousand-square-foot store was constructed on the former site of the Windsor Hotel in 1955, sharing a building with F.W. Woolworth. *Courtesy of the Jacksonville Public Library Special Collections Department.*

served as the stockroom, retail sales took place at street level and the second floor housed executive offices and the kitchen. The five and dime store was located right next to JCPenney, and they shared a common wall where one could literally walk from one to the other without going outside. Behind them was the twenty-one-story Robert Meyer Hotel; together, the three establishments occupied an entire city block.

Prior to moving to the Hemming Park location in May 1955, JCPenney had been located in a smaller building at the intersection of Main and Bay Streets since opening in Jacksonville in 1933. JCPenney began with the opening of James Cash Penney's "The Golden Rule" store in 1902 in Kemmerer, Wyoming. In 1913, the company was incorporated under the new name J.C. Penney Company, with William Henry McManus as a co-founder. In 1914, the headquarters was moved to New York City to simplify the buying, financing and transportation of goods. By 1917, the company operated 175 stores in twenty-two states in the United States. The company opened its 500th store in 1924 in Hamilton, Missouri, James Cash Penney's hometown. By the opening of the 1,000th store in 1928, gross business had reached $190 million.

The Robert Meyer Hotel was the final component of the JCPenney/F.W. Woolworth complex. Standing twenty-one stories tall, the hotel was the brainchild of owner Jack Meyer of Alabama, a former World War II Flying Tigers squadron pilot. Breaking ground in 1957, the hotel was named for Meyer's father and brother, who were both named Robert. The $6 million, 563-room tower was the first hotel to be constructed in Jacksonville in thirty-two years and Florida's largest hotel at the time of its grand opening on March 22, 1959. Helping anchor the Hemming Park retail environment established by Cohen Brothers Big Store, the 215-foot-tall hotel was said to have everything, including a block-long marble lobby and tropical garden, a jewelry store, a rooftop pool, a cabana deck, three restaurants, a cocktail lounge and a two-level, 190-space underground parking garage.

Sears, Roebuck and Company

In 1956, the Sears, Roebuck and Company made a huge splash into downtown Jacksonville's retail market with acquisition of the Seaboard Coastline Railroad's downtown freight station, yard and divisional offices. At the time, Sears' demographics indicated that Jacksonville was spreading mainly in three directions from downtown. In the event that a downtown store site was not located, the alternative option would have been to construct three smaller stores outside of Springfield, Riverside and in the Southside.

The $1 million purchase of eight and a half acres along the St. Johns Riverfront would anchor a development pattern that would forever change the face and economy of downtown Jacksonville. Prior to the 1950s, downtown Jacksonville's economy had been anchored by being a location where the railroad and maritime industries met. This interchange led to the clustering of a mix of uses, industries and complementing services that spurred the development of downtown's red-light, retail and tourism industries. In addition, these core industries employed thousands of Jaxsons within a compact downtown setting. For example, the Jacksonville Terminal Company employed over two thousand workers during this era.

With downtown's retail sector booming, Sears decided to build the "Cadillac of Sears stores in the South." To make room for the store and its seven-hundred-space surface parking lot, Seaboard Coastline's railroad freight station and divisional offices were demolished and relocated to Warrington Avenue in the neighborhood of Lackawanna on the Westside of Jacksonville. In addition, several Seaboard Coastline tenants—including the Union Bus Terminal, Tyler Produce Company, New York Terminal Warehouse Company and the Swift Company—were forced to either close or relocate their activities from the site. Furthermore, to facilitate the development of the new store, Julia Street was abandoned and closed between the river and Bay Street.

An aerial of Sears' Cadillac store at the intersection of Hogan and Bay Streets as it appeared in 1962. Dominating the background, the Big Store can be seen in the center of the aerial. *Courtesy of the State Archives of Florida.*

Demolition of Seaboard Coastline's rail facilities took place in 1957 for a department store that was envisioned to be the best. The store was the brainchild of Charles Kelstadt, then the head of Sears' southeastern territory and later to become the chairman of the board. When completed in June 1959, it was considered an innovative creation for the department store industry nationwide. The Cadillac store's unique features included the largest auto accessory department in the nation. It was also the first department store to have a sit-down restaurant with waiter service instead of cafeteria style, the last Sears store built with more than two floors and the first urban department store to have a surface parking lot of its own. When it opened in June 1959, the store quickly became the cream of Sears' crop, featuring 260,000 square feet of retail space spread out over four levels and a basement. It attracted over forty thousand shoppers for its opening day.

Retired transportation consultant Robert Mann recalls that some of his fondest childhood memories of downtown Jacksonville were of the Sears candy and nut counter:

> *As for the candy and nut counter, as I recall it was an island near one of the entries to the store. I don't know how or where they came from but those big bulk glass boxes held the sweetest cashews, peanuts, walnuts, and pecans in the world, and scented the entire store with a sweet perfume. You'd walk in and ZAP that sweet scent would attack your senses and the visuals became irresistible. The concept was brilliant because today's big box stores smell like a combination of stale popcorn, body odor and cheap floor cleaner.*

To some degree, the place operated as a mini-mall. In addition to the usual departments, separate shops existed for pets, hobbies, gifts, tobacco, cameras, health products and Boy and Girl Scout items. Other features included a watch and jewelry repair service, a beauty salon called the Lyric and a home furnishings center with four decorating consultants who gave advice in the store or at one's home. Two comfortable rooms also allowed customers to listen to records and radios in soundproof surroundings. And Sears heeded the needs of harried moms with tots under school age. While their mothers shopped, little baby boomers could be left at a free nursery supervised by a registered nurse.

Sears patrons dined on one of the specialties of the Jean Ribault Room: shrimp salad served in an abalone pearl shell. This in-store restaurant, clad in cool, calming greens, was situated on the second floor. It indicated its First Coast location through a thirty-three-foot-long mural by Jax artist Lee Adams. The painting depicted the 1562 landing of Frenchman Jean Ribault at the mouth of the St. Johns River. Appropriately, coffee was served to diners by two girls in sixteenth-century French costumes. Patrons could also frequent the building's Peggy Kellogg coffee shop. As one website visitor notes about this eatery, "I remember going in as a child and my parents would get me a chocolate milk drink."

Standing at the corner of Bay and Pearl Streets was a mammoth Sears automotive center, which serviced thirty vehicles at a time. Customers could also take advantage of a copious garden center. This was connected to the main structure by a covered walkway and a bridge over a reflecting pool. All in all, the entire Sears complex was staffed by over 1,100 employees.

Chapter 7

Changing Demographics

Suburban Explosion

Shortly after the successful opening of Victor David Gruen's Southdale Mall in Minnesota, major department stores began looking to expand outside of downtown Jacksonville and into rapidly growing suburban areas of Duval County. Gruen was an Austrian-born architect best known as the pioneer in the design of shopping malls in the United States. An advocate of prioritizing pedestrians over cars in urban cores, Gruen would become the designer of the Kalamazoo Mall, the first outdoor pedestrian mall in the country, in downtown Kalamazoo in 1958.

Gruen, who described suburbia as being "soulless" and "in search of a heart," saw the mall as a method to create better versions of the American downtown in outlying areas. Gruen's vision called for the enclosed mall to become a civic center as much as a commercial complex by featuring day cares, libraries, post offices, community halls and public art. Little did he know that his idea would set off a chain reaction that would forever change the atmosphere, context, economic structure and density of downtowns across America. His first suburban shopping center was an open-air facility called Northland Mall near Detroit in 1954. Soon he was hired by the owners of Dayton Department stores to design the 800,000-square-foot Southdale Mall in Edina, Minnesota. Southdale opened its doors in 1956 to seventy-five thousand shoppers, becoming the first modern enclosed suburban mall in the country. Southdale did an amazing job of luring in customers and holding them captive in the shopping bliss now known as the Gruen Effect. Florida's first shopping mall was Fort Lauderdale's

An aerial view of the Arlington Plaza shopping center at the intersection of Arlington Road and Arlington Expressway in 1957. With the opening of the Mathews Bridge in 1953, Arlington became one of Jacksonville's most rapidly growing suburbs through the 1960s, leading to the construction of Regency Square Mall. *Courtesy of the State Archives of Florida, Robert E. Fisher Collection.*

Sunrise Center, which opened as an open-air center in January 1954. Orlando's Colonial Plaza was the first enclosed shopping center in Florida, opening in October 1962. Within a year, the concept of the enclosed mall in suburbia would come to Jacksonville.

On November 16, 1957, it was announced that Food Fair Properties had exercised an option to purchase a 43.5-acre tract of land for $600,000 on Jacksonville's Southside for the construction of Jacksonville's first enclosed mall and the Southeast's largest shopping center to date. According to Thomas R. Smith of New York, a mortgage broker who helped negotiate the Food Fair deal, "Jacksonville was the natural center of Florida and could be a center for the whole Southeast area." The project offered Food Fair an opportunity to locate a regional shopping center in Jacksonville in order to tie its operations outside of the state with another company

Opening in 1962, Orlando's Colonial Plaza was the first enclosed mall in Florida. *Courtesy of Malls of America.*

property, 163rd Street Shopping Center, in Miami. At the time, the mall's intended anchors included Montgomery Ward and two department stores that failed to materialize into actual leases, Saks Fifth Avenue and Richards Department Store.

Called Philips Mall, the 400,000-square-foot shopping center opened in November 1960 at the intersection of Philips Highway and Emerson Street, bordering Jacksonville's city limits two and a half miles south of downtown. Original plans indicated that the $7 million center, which was designed by New York architect Lathrop Douglass, would lease 60 percent of its space to national chains and that total employment generated would be three thousand. The site was selected because pending construction of a new expressway (Interstate 95) would put the location within a ten-minute drive of any spot in Greater Jacksonville. New to the Jacksonville retail scene was Montgomery Ward, which constructed a $2.5 million, 121,800-square-foot department store along frontage facing the proposed expressway. Montgomery Ward's two-story structure, along with J.M. Fields and Woolworths, served as the anchor for the mall's fifty specialty stores.

Ten days after the Philips Mall announcement on November 29, 1957, Guy W. Luke, manager of the downtown JCPenney store, held a press release to announce the construction of his company's first 45,000-square-foot suburban Jacksonville stores intended for the Northside's proposed North Gate Plaza and Cedar Hills Shopping Center on Blanding Boulevard in Cedar Hills. The Northside development became known as Gateway Shopping Center when it officially opened in 1959 as an open-air strip retail center. Designed in the shape of an upside-down L, the shopping center was initially anchored by the region's first JCPenney store outside of downtown Jacksonville, W.T. Grant, G.C. Murphy, Food Fair and Winn-Dixie. The second suburban branch opened a few years later in May 1961 in a 66,100-square-foot space in Cedar Hills. One of Jacksonville's early suburban communities after World War II, Cedar Hills was a rapidly growing area featuring ranch-style single-family homes just southwest of the city along the Cedar River. Several streets in the neighborhood were named with a thematic muse in mind, including Mother Goose Road, Peter Pan Place and the rabbit warren of Flopsy, Mopsy and Cotton Tail Lanes. Like Gateway Shopping Center, the 282,000-square-foot Cedar Hills Shopping Center was an early forerunner to Victor Gruen's enclosed regional mall concept in Jacksonville when it was originally completed in 1955.

With the Downtown Center joint-venture development with May-Cohens underway, Robert H. Jacobs turned his company's sights to Jacksonville's growing suburbs. On February 20, 1960, Jacobs announced his intentions to develop a $2.5 million shopping center just north of the Ortega River on a twenty-acre site bordering Roosevelt Boulevard. Named Roosevelt Mall, the development would launch the Cohen Brothers' longtime competitor, Furchgott's, into suburban expansion with a thirty-thousand-square-foot branch department store anchoring the open-air shopping center, which was completed in 1961. Although Furchgott's opened a branch store at 160 North Beach Street in downtown Daytona Beach on November 1, 1956, the Roosevelt Mall store was the company's first in Jacksonville outside of downtown. At the mall's opening ceremonies, Jacobs told the crowd that "we have made Roosevelt Mall something more than just another shopping center." Indeed, Jacobs had constructed what was considered an ultimate shopping center. It featured pools at either end of the walkways, both containing a pair of swans, and a forty-five-foot abstract sculpture created by Andre Bloc of Paris at the mall's center court. Retired transportation consultant Robert Mann recalled his thoughts about Roosevelt Mall as a young child: "Roosevelt Mall took the prize in beauty indoors or outdoors, depending on which era one refers to. To this day, in my opinion, it was far more artistic, tropical, artsy, than any other North Florida Mall."

In May 1963, during a luncheon at the nearby Robert Meyer Hotel, Montgomery Ward announced that it would open its second suburban department store in Jacksonville, making the city the only municipality in Florida with two of the chain's stores. The new store would be five and a half miles west of downtown Jacksonville. This $2.6 million department store would anchor Edward J. DeBartolo Corporation's Normandy Mall. The mall was the second enclosed mall to be developed by DeBartolo. Located near the intersection of Normandy Boulevard and Cassat Avenue on Jacksonville's Westside, this enclosed shopping center would replace the former thirty-seven-acre Normandy Drive-In Theatre. The 462,284-square-foot shopping center opened by the end of 1963, becoming Jacksonville's first fully enclosed mall and Florida's second to be built as a fully enclosed structure. Previously an open-air center, Orlando's Colonial Plaza was the first enclosed shopping center in Florida, opening in October 1962. By the end of that year, Fort Lauderdale's Coral Ridge Plaza had opened, becoming the state's first fully enclosed shopping mall. Anchored by the 134,000-square-foot Montgomery Ward and 1,836 parking spaces, Normandy Mall also featured a 31,700-square-foot North Carolina–based P.H. Rose variety store and a one-thousand-seat twin theater operated by Kent Theatres. Other

Twenty-five thousand shoppers flooded the doors of Martin Stein's Regency Square Mall—billing itself as the largest shopping center in the Southeast—when it opened in 1967. *Courtesy of the State Archives of Florida.*

stores in the enclosed mall included a Food Fair supermarket, Gray's Drug Store, Vogue Shops, Kay's Jewelers, Edward's Men's and Boys' Shop and a Stand 'N' Snack.

In 1965, three years after opening its massive downtown Jacksonville store, J.B. Ivey & Company announced its plans for a smaller thirty-thousand-square-foot second Jacksonville store to be located at the proposed Regency Square Mall. The Regency store opened in 1967, and the chain followed this expansion with the addition of a twenty-seven-thousand-square-foot store at Lake Shore's Roosevelt Square Mall in 1968. According to Ivey's officials, the success of the Regency Square Mall store was the major reason for the expansion of the chain's second store outside of downtown Jacksonville.

Chapter 8

The Big Store Heads to the Suburbs

With the May Company's acquisition of Cohen Brothers in 1959, the company began to evaluate the Jacksonville market for the expansion of stores in rapidly growing suburban areas. Upon entering the Jacksonville market, Morton Jay May had been quick to mention that the company was the first large department store to go suburban with the opening of a Los Angeles branch store in 1938. However, in the first half of the 1960s, May-Cohens had been the last of the large downtown Jacksonville department stores to expand outside the urban core. By this time, the once isolated Big Store was surrounded by J.B. Ivey's, JCPenney and Woolworth; Hemming Park had become the cultural epicenter of Jacksonville. A few blocks away were Levy's, Furchgott's and Sears, all with brand-new branch stores outside downtown Jacksonville performing well and gaining market share.

Regency Square Mall, 1967

With downtown's grasp on the Jacksonville retail market rapidly losing ground to the city's booming suburbs and regional malls, May-Cohens finally decided to follow the lead of neighboring department stores by expanding outside of downtown itself. Opportunity for suburban expansion would present itself for May-Cohens in 1965 with the announcement by

Now operating as Belk, this department store was the first branch of May-Cohens to open outside downtown Jacksonville. *Courtesy of the author.*

husband-and-wife developers Martin E. and Joan Wellhouse Stein of their intention to construct one of the nation's largest and most modern enclosed-mall shopping centers in Arlington on a sixty-acre site strip-mined by Humphreys Gold for titanium. The Steins' Regency Square Mall would cost $12 million to construct and add 602,940 square feet of retail space to the expanding Jacksonville retail market. Designed as a regional center catering to all of northeast Florida, the mall's location was situated on the north side of Arlington Expressway where Atlantic Boulevard and the expressway merged to go to the beaches.

Groundbreaking for the mall opened with a champagne breakfast at the Thunderbird Inn, where 175 prominent Jacksonville businessmen, including Florida governor Haydon Burns, had gathered as the invited guests of Mr. and Mrs. Stein. At the event, Mayor Louis H. Ritter praised the Steins for their contributions to the city. "They are giving us the great things we need to make the Jacksonville area a regional center," Ritter stated.

The Steins commissioned the architecture firm of Toombs, Amisano & Wells to design Regency Square Mall. The Steins believed they had picked the best firm available because it had recently designed Atlanta's Lenox Square. Mrs. Stein was determined to get top-notch anchors for their project. The first to agree was JCPenney, which was already seeking an expansion site where multiple highways converged. May-Cohens would follow JCPenney with plans for an 115,991-square-foot department store anchoring the mall's west end. Soon, Furchgott's, Levy's, Ivey's and F.W. Woolworth would follow because they believed the mall was too good of an opportunity to pass up.

Regency Square Mall opened its doors on Thursday, March 1, 1967, billing itself as the largest shopping center in the Southeast. It touted its convenience with advertising that read, "All roads lead to Regency Square." Grand opening ceremonies were held at 9:45 a.m. at the mall's main arcade, which was blocked by a golden chain that was opened by the Steins. Mayor Ritter, County Commissioner Bob Harris and W. Ashley Verlander of the Jacksonville Area Chamber of Commerce took part in the opening ceremonies. Traffic on the Arlington Expressway came to a standstill as an estimated twenty-five thousand shoppers flooded the mall on opening day.

Roosevelt Mall, 1972

With the successful opening of the Regency Square Mall branch store, May-Cohens turned its attention to Jacksonville's Westside. Roosevelt Mall, which originally opened in 1961, was fresh off the heels of a major renovation project that converted the open-air shopping center into a fully air-conditioned, enclosed mall. This $1 million expansion project was completed in August 1968, a year after the opening of Regency Square Mall on the other side of the city. The centerpiece of the expansion and renovation project was the development of Jacksonville's third J.B. Ivey & Company department store. This 29,000-square-foot store joined F.W. Woolworth and Furchgott's as the mall's main anchors. May-Cohens became the mall's third and largest anchor as part of an expansion of the mall's south esplanade, opening in November 1972. The addition of May-Cohens' 33,785-square-foot branch store increased the overall square footage of the shopping center to 243,217 square feet.

In 1972, May-Cohens opened what would remain the smallest store in the growing chain at Jacksonville's Roosevelt Mall. *Courtesy of the author.*

VOLUSIA MALL, 1974

In 1974, May-Cohens' outward expansion resulted in the opening of a new store in Daytona Beach, Florida. The $5 million store would be an anchor for Edward J. DeBartolo Corporation's proposed Volusia Mall, which was officially announced in February 1973. Intended for a ninety-three-acre site north of Daytona International Speedway, DeBartolo estimated that when in full operation, it would employ at least two thousand people.

In unveiling plans for the two-level, 100,000-square-foot store, Alvin Richer, president of May-Cohens, expressed confidence that the September 1974 target date set for its opening would be met. It was said that no expense would be spared in making the Daytona Beach store the most beautiful department store in all of Florida. Designed to stress traditional elegance, the interior of the store was envisioned as the prototype of future May-Cohens expansion in Florida. According to Richer, "Our aim is to create a

The year 1974 would see the expansion of the May-Cohens chain into central Florida with a 100,000-square-foot store at Daytona Beach's Volusia Mall. *Courtesy of the State Archives of Florida.*

quiet, friendly atmosphere that will make shopping at May-Cohens Daytona Beach a unique and pleasurable experience."

Designed by Newport Beach, California–based Ladd & Kelsey Architects, the store's first floor was devoted to clothing apparel for the entire family. The second floor featured home accessories and furniture departments. In addition, the second floor included a restaurant and gourmet food and wine shop in a country store setting. Volusia Mall opened on October 14, 1974. The 820,000-square-foot shopping center was one of three Florida malls opened by Edward DeBartolo in 1974. The other two were Altamonte Mall on August 1 and University Square in Tampa on August 15. It was anchored by May-Cohens, Sears, JCPenney and Ivey's, but Ivey's 123,000-square-foot store was the only anchor to open along with the mall. May-Cohens officially opened a couple of months later in December 1974 to a crowd of two hundred people surging through its doors. It would be joined by a 200,000-square-foot Sears in February 1975 and a 144,000-square-foot JCPenney in August 1975. May-Cohens' decision to open a store at Volusia Square Mall wasn't the chain's first time considering expanding into the Daytona Beach market. A few years earlier, it was envisioned that May-Cohens would be the second anchor at South Daytona's Sunshine Mall. Anchored by a Woolco, that 255,000-square-foot shopping center opened on September 30, 1970, 3.3 miles south of downtown Daytona Beach.

Orange Park Mall, 1975

May-Cohens' expansion outside of Duval County would continue in 1975 with the opening of a 99,166-square-foot store in Clay County's Orange Park Mall. With its opening, Orange Park Mall would briefly hold the moniker as the largest enclosed shopping mall in the Jacksonville metropolitan area, surpassing Gateway Center and Regency Square Mall. Developed by Cousins Properties, Inc. of Atlanta, Georgia, the 751,490-square-foot shopping mall opened in September 1975 with May-Cohens, Sears and Ivey's as anchors and 4,614 free parking spaces for its visitors. Furchgott's also expanded its chain with a smaller 20,000-square-foot branch store at Orange Park Mall. Located on a one-hundred-acre property at Blanding Boulevard and Wells Road, the shopping mall cost $37 million to construct. Fifteen hundred guests were invited to the mall's ribbon-cutting ceremony, which featured May-Cohens' president, Alvin Richer, as a keynote speaker. At the event, Richer would proclaim:

According to May-Cohens' president, Alvin Richer, the opening of a branch at Clay County's Orange Park Mall in 1975 was a further manifestation of the company's confidence in north Florida. *Courtesy of the author.*

May Cohens is a 108-year-old Florida institution dedicated to the principles of fashion, quality, integrity and service. May Cohens Orange Park is a further manifestation of our confidence in the fast growing North Florida area. I believe the decor and appointments throughout the new store will altogether create a quiet, friendly, inviting atmosphere that will make shopping here a truly unique and pleasurable experience.

Gateway Center, 1978

May-Cohens would open its fifth and final store in Jacksonville with the addition of a store at Gateway Center in September 1978. The company's latest location took the place of Gateway's W.T. Grant. W.T. Grant, an original anchor at Gateway Shopping Center, closed in 1976 as the chain succumbed in the second-largest bankruptcy in U.S. history at the time. With

The Northside's Gateway Center May-Cohens branch closed its doors in 1988. The building, shown here in 2012, still sits empty. *Courtesy of the author.*

the addition of May-Cohens and a forty-thousand-square-foot expansion of specialty retail, Gateway reached its peak as a Jacksonville retail destination. At the time, in addition to May-Cohens, the shopping center featured JCPenney, Service Merchandise and Jefferson Ward as its anchor stores.

Chapter 9

A Mall for the Big Store

During the 1960s, 2.7 million square feet of floor space was added to the Jacksonville retail market by general merchandisers. The lion's share of this growth took place outside of the downtown Jacksonville retail scene that the May-Cohens' Big Store had stimulated nearly sixty years earlier. This growth had a significant negative impact on the health of downtown Jacksonville's retail environment. In 1962, the year after Roosevelt Mall opened, a market survey conducted by WJXT of area shopping habits indicated that 55 percent of the local population shopped predominantly downtown, while the remaining 45 percent favored suburban centers. By the end of the decade, major expansions by Roosevelt Mall and Gateway Shopping Center, coupled with the addition of Normandy and Regency Square Malls, had increased the suburban share to 75 percent while reducing downtown's market share to 25 percent. When asked "Why do you do the majority of your shopping for products other than groceries, drugs and convenience goods at a shopping center?" 97 percent of respondents cited free and easier parking as the major reason. An additional 33 percent complained about downtown traffic. When asked "What things do you think could be done to improve downtown shopping?" 84 percent of the responses suggested improving the parking situation and parking prices. Furthermore, the study confirmed that downtown's most consistent department store shoppers were homemakers ages fifty and over and/or with low family incomes. Other significant data suggested that the local population favored suburban shopping centers for smaller items such as clothing and linens, while they favored traveling to downtown to purchase furniture and appliances.

By the 1970s, downtown had become a decaying district suffering from many of the same factors that decimated urban cities throughout the United States, such as white flight, racism and blight. In addition, with a draconian parking meter situation, toll bridges and the proliferation of suburban shopping options, a potent combination for the failure of the once vibrant downtown retail market had been established.

At the time, city officials and economists believed that the future of downtown Jacksonville's retail market would be heavily influenced by what was accomplished, or not accomplished, to make it competitive with the large new shopping centers springing up in the suburbs. This line of thinking led to the creation of the 1971 Downtown Master Plan, a dramatic improvement plan and program intended to give downtown the amenities that already flourished in the suburban shopping malls. Rogers, Taliaferro, Kostritsky, and Lamb (RTKL) of Baltimore was hired by the Downtown Development Authority to develop this revitalization plan intended to save the Big Store and its neighbors. Founded in 1946 by Archibald Rogers and Francis Taliaferro in Rogers' grandmother's basement in Annapolis, Maryland, RTKL was known for its impressive work on the Charles Center area in downtown Baltimore. RTKL believed downtown revitalization would be most effective by transforming the area into a mall-like environment to help rejuvenate retail sales in an area that was continuing to hemorrhage from the competition of popular suburban malls like Regency, Gateway, Roosevelt, Philips and Normandy.

RTKL's plan for downtown Jacksonville evolved around three major features. The first was a vehicular and pedestrian public circulation system. The second was focusing on concentrated and mixed-use land activities, and the third was to create a new landmark symbolizing the revitalization of downtown Jacksonville. The RTKL plan was legally adopted on January 12, 1971, by the Jacksonville City Council. It called for concentrating the most intensive office and retail uses to occur within the heart of the downtown core. These uses would then be organized around a public circulation system that would be composed of pedestrian and vehicular networks. The vehicular circulation plan called for developing a new loop system where vehicular traffic would be routed around the heart of the Northbank, helping convert the core of downtown into a large pedestrian mall. The loop system consisted of converting Water, Ocean, Beaver and Pearl Streets into a one-way outer loop, while turning Main, Ashley, Julia and Bay Streets into a

After sixty years of operating at Hemming Park, changing demographics had begun to take their toll on the visual appeal of the Big Store and the surrounding retail district to the average Jacksonville shopper. *Courtesy of the City of Jacksonville Historic Preservation Office.*

The confusing network of one-way streets in downtown Jacksonville today was part of the 1971 plan to transform the Big Store and the surrounding Hemming Park retail district into a pedestrian mall to compete with the popularity of Jacksonville's suburban shopping centers. *Courtesy of the Jacksonville Public Library Special Collections Department.*

one-way inner loop. Parking garages and surface lots containing at least five thousand spaces would then be constructed along the loop streets to provide downtown with a competitive amount of parking that was a common feature at area shopping malls.

The pedestrian component would eliminate pedestrian-vehicular conflicts by creating a continuous walkway system throughout the core of Jacksonville's central business district. Anchored by two urban parks—Hemming Park to the north and a proposed riverfront park to the south—the pedestrian circulation network would have been formed by a series of urban parks, malls, arcades, elevated walkways and plazas.

The third essential feature of the RTKL plan for the revitalization of downtown Jacksonville was the creation of a new park and cultural and recreational complex along the St. Johns River. It was envisioned that this development would serve as an impressive image and a functional symbol of the rebirth of the downtown market that the Cohen Brothers Big Store had played a significant role in establishing.

Under RTKL's proposal, Hogan and Laura Streets, between Church and Bay Streets, would be transformed into pedestrian malls. These malls were envisioned as streets where pedestrian traffic would be given partial or total priority over all other forms of mobility and traffic. Surrounded by the roadway loop system, the pedestrian mall was proposed to be divided into three major segments: the New Riverfront Center, the Laura/Hogan Axis and the Retail Core Area.

The Riverfront Center area would be the southern focal point of the pedestrian mall concept developed by RTKL. It would include a riverfront park, convention hotel, exhibition center and vertical financial-office complex bridging over Bay Street, all developed around Sears' existing "Cadillac" store. The Laura/Hogan Axis would serve as a retail connector and pedestrian zone between the River Center Area to the south and the Retail Core Area surrounding Hemming Park. A major element of the Laura/Hogan Axis was the Atlantic Bank Complex. At the time, the bank had plans to construct a new headquarters tower at the intersection of Forsyth and Hogan Streets. Once completed, its old headquarters complex, which was adjacent to Furchgott's, would be converted into a retail entertainment complex featuring a movie theater and retail arcade within the historic Atlantic Bank Building. To further separate pedestrians from vehicular traffic, a system of elevated walkways would be emphasized, stretching from the river to the Cathedral Apartments off Ocean Street.

At the heart of the redevelopment plan was Hemming Park and May-Cohens' Big Store. Dating back to early 1970, the city council and the Jacksonville chapter of the American Institute of Architects desired to rejuvenate the park so that it would become more enjoyed than feared. With this in mind, the architectural firm of Fisher, Broward, Shepard and Coons unveiled plans for converting the park into an urban-oriented plaza in January 1970. The purpose of the redesign was to create a space where residents would be proud of a situation where that space would generate redevelopment in the heart of downtown. As part of the redesign, trees would be removed because they were viewed as too tall and skinny and could not be enjoyed from ground level.

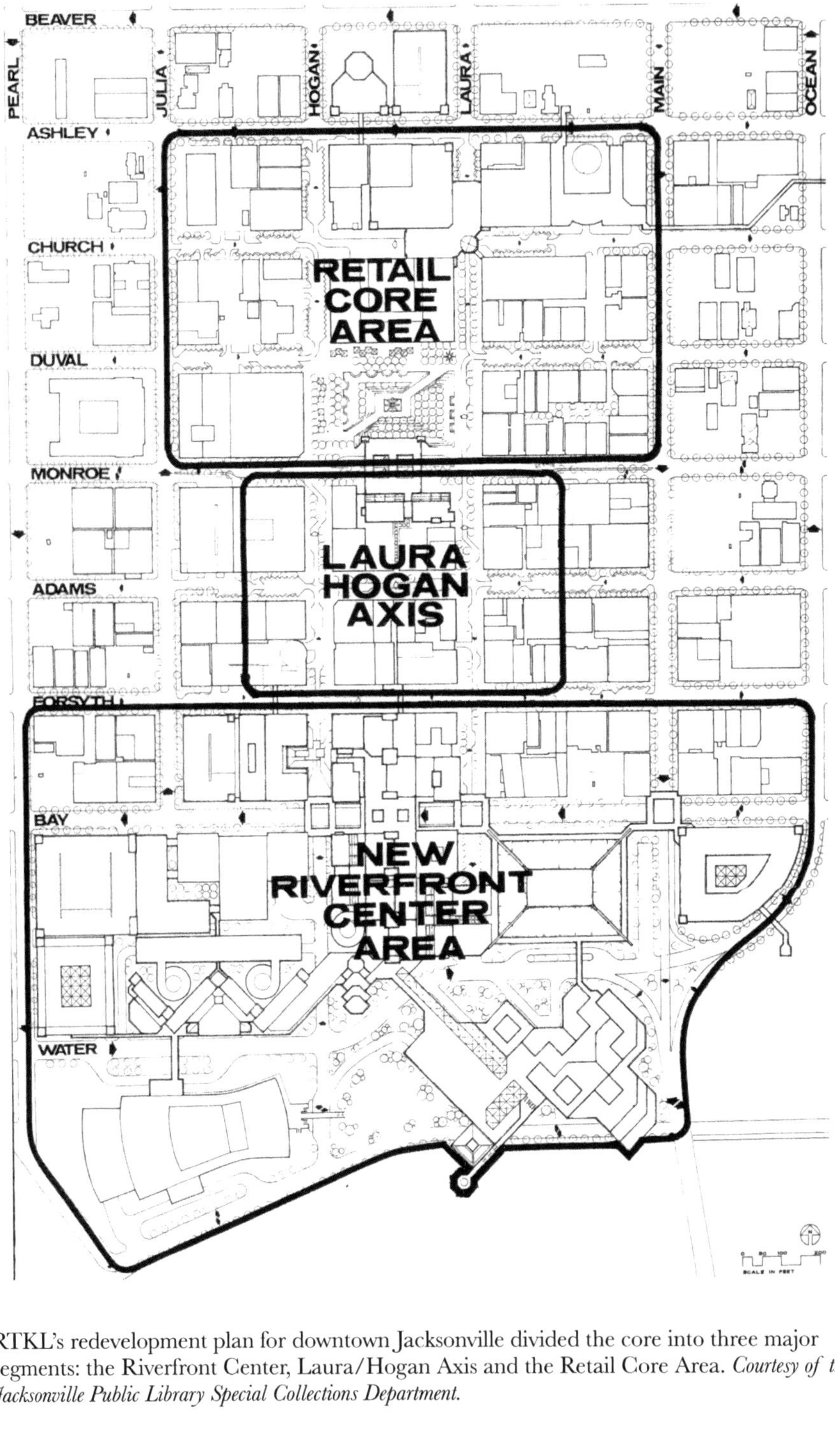

RTKL's redevelopment plan for downtown Jacksonville divided the core into three major segments: the Riverfront Center, Laura/Hogan Axis and the Retail Core Area. *Courtesy of the Jacksonville Public Library Special Collections Department.*

A sketch of the enclosed multi-level retail galleria intended to connect the Big Store with neighboring Ivey's department store and Purcell's women's store. *Courtesy of the Jacksonville Public Library Special Collections Department.*

Within RTKL's 1971 Master Plan, this concept became the basis of the Retail Core Area. Here, Hemming Park would become a central plaza for the pedestrian mall and transit terminal for the Jacksonville Transportation Authority bus system. However, the most unique feature of the Retail Core Area would be the construction of an elevated, enclosed retail galleria mall utilizing the May-Cohens' Big Store as an anchor.

Elevated above the intersection of Laura and Church Streets, the four-story galleria was seen as a unique retail solution within a United States urban environment. It would be developed in air rights above the streets to connect May-Cohens' flagship store, Ivey's and Purcell's to a common parking garage just north of May-Cohens. The galleria would then serve as an enclosed mall featuring multiple levels of specialty shops to complement the three large existing anchors. The central feature of the galleria was envisioned to be a sky-lighted interior public gallery around which vertical and horizontal circulation would be organized. RTKL's opinion was that this concept would provide three critical things for the downtown retail market: an enclosed, environmentally controlled mall connecting major department

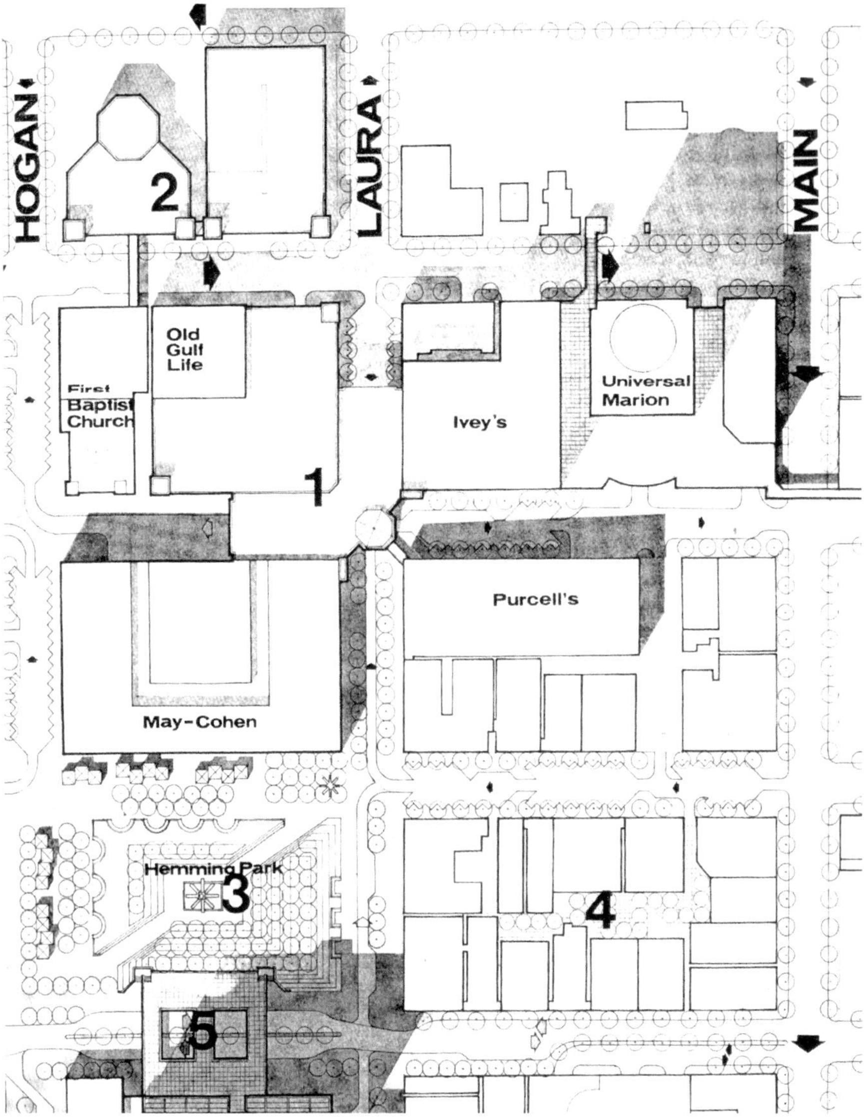

A plan view of the concept to construct an elevated retail shopping galleria to tie the Big Store (May Cohen), Ivey's and Purcell's together with a neighboring parking garage. It was believed that a mall in the heart of downtown would turn the Hemming Park area around. *Courtesy of the Jacksonville Public Library Special Collections Department.*

stores, convenient parking and a security-controlled environment for shoppers. With the galleria mall in place, the pedestrian circulation network would provide direct pedestrian-only connectivity between May-Cohens and JCPenney, Levy-Wolf, Furchgott's and Sears, all of which happened to share frontage on Hogan Street. While dreaming up ways to save downtown Jacksonville's retail sector from dying had been accomplished, the reality of actually implementing the plan would prove to become a daunting task.

By 1976, Morrison's Cafeteria, which faced May-Cohens on the other side of Hemming Park, had closed, and neighboring Ivey's had shuttered two floors in its six-story building. However, Don Ingram, executive director of the downtown development authority, pointed out that the Ivey's closing was based on a company policy throughout the Southeast and not the downtown business environment and that while Morrison's had closed, two new restaurants had opened. According to Ingram, things were looking up for downtown: "Since 1968 there has been a 25% increase in the number of people working in downtown and Jacksonville has one of the most stable downtown areas, for a city of its size, in the nation." In an editorial to the *Florida Times-Union*, Michael Lissner, president of the Downtown Merchants Association, proclaimed:

> *Where do women go when they want to buy quality fashion merchandise? Downtown. Where do men go when they want to see a selection of suits? Downtown. I could name a lot of other areas where downtown is the only place to really get a selection. Jewelry, luggage, home furnishings, ladies shoes, are just a few of the obvious ones.*
>
> *There's been a rash of sensationalized articles about Downtown. You know, there's no place that you can't find a little dirt if that's what you're looking for. You'll find a roach in the most immaculate house. I'm sure there was plenty of poison ivy in the Garden of Eden.*

Even growth projects of the era supported this line of thinking. Projections indicated that by 1990, 18,000 people would be living in downtown, which only had a residential population of 158 in 1975. By the same token, in 1970 the old city limits of Jacksonville contained 164,739 residents. Projections indicated that number would increase to 182,500 by 1990.

With optimism abound, by early November 1976, the Big Store and several of its neighboring merchants had banded together and launched the "Downtown Discovery Days" promotion campaign in hopes of starting a rejuvenation of the downtown retail market. At the Big Store, plans were made for a "Breakfast with Santa" program. Next door, JCPenney was in the process of wrapping up a major renovation of its store for a November 18 grand opening in time for the Christmas season. According to manager Jim Stout, the first two floors had been completely revamped, and "the store was placing a strong emphasis on fashion." On the other side of the Big Store, Ivey's made plans for its annual Christmas Eve eggnog party. There, the Christmas cheer was passed around for late shoppers and employees from 4:00 p.m. until Christmas closing time at 6:00 p.m. Down the street at Furchgott's, manager Richard Sadowsky claimed that he was looking forward to having a good season and that his store was already feeling the benefits from the Downtown Discovery Days promotion program. Overall, merchants believed the campaign effort increased their sales by 20 to 30 percent.

Despite the optimism, some felt a different way. "I like the job opportunities downtown, but I have to pay tolls to get here and a fortune in parking," said Sam Frio, a May-Cohens salesman. For nearby Phelps Fabrics manager Bob Mays, parking was a major problem: "The big problem downtown is parking. I had a lady come in the store with a parking ticket…she was so mad she threw it on the table and said, 'Here, this is yours.'"

After the 1976 Christmas season, downtown's retail environment continued its downward trend. Despite opening to great fanfare, downtown's changing demographics placed the grand Robert Meyer Hotel into financial problems, leading to the hotel closing in bankruptcy in August 1977. Struggling to survive in a declining downtown market, the hotel filed for reorganization under the Federal Bankruptcy Act on June 1, 1977. Under the bankruptcy plan, the hotel had to maintain its current payments until a reorganization plan could be set up to pay off $2 million in back debts. Initially, heavy convention traffic kept the hotel afloat, but by July, the business started to slack off, and by August, no additional conventions had been scheduled. After its abrupt closing, nearly 100 former workers showed up to collect their final paychecks, but police cleared the lobby area and locked the doors. Later, bankruptcy judge George Proctor ordered that the hotel's remaining cash be used to make partial payment of the $22,000 payroll owed to the 150-employee workforce.

By the end of 1977, a plan developed by Jacksonville-based KBJ Architects called for the park to be transformed into an urban plaza with a goal for better pedestrian circulation and visibility and less bus traffic. This would serve as the first phase of RTKL's 1971 Master Plan. In 1978, when work on the revamp of Hemming Park finally began, optimism for a revitalized

During the late 1970s, the increasing popularity of Regency Square and Orange Park Malls wreaked havoc on the Big Store and downtown retail market. Thousands of cars consume the expansive parking lot of Orange Park Mall shortly after its 1975 opening. *Courtesy of the Jacksonville Public Library Special Collections Department.*

downtown was at its height. According to Robert Cockayne, president of May-Cohens and chairman of the Downtown Development Council of the Jacksonville Area Chamber of Commerce, even the downtown May-Cohens store was in the midst of experiencing a "turn-around" in business following a slump that had plagued the central business district for the better part of seven to eight years. In conjunction with the renovation of storefronts on Hogan and Laura Streets, it was envisioned that the mall-like shopping setting highlighted in the 1971 Downtown Master Plan was finally on its way to becoming reality.

Nevertheless, while plans were being drawn up for a mall-like setting around the Big Store, suburban malls like Regency Square continued to rake in the cash. According to an Urban Land Institute study, by 1979, Regency Square had become one of the most profitable shopping centers in the nation. While the average sales per square foot downtown was $88, Regency was bringing in $156.

Chapter 10

An Icon Vanishes

Implementation of the 1971 plan was a very slow process. First, seven years of planning and working to obtain funding had taken place before the conversion of Hemming Park into a plaza got underway. During that time, the region's newest mall, Orange Park Mall, had been proposed, constructed and completed, further pulling suburban growth into Clay County. Also, due to increased competition from Regency Square Mall and other suburban centers, Gateway Shopping Center had expanded as well in 1978 with forty thousand square feet of new retail. Both projects included May-Cohens branch stores of their own.

The KBJ-designed renovation of Hemming Park into an urban plaza was intended to be the downtown pedestrian mall's first phase. This reconstruction of Hemming Plaza was completed in time for the Big Store's 1978 Christmas season for $648,000. However, the $2.2 million second phase, which would involve closing streets and changing the traffic directional flow, was continually delayed and postponed for a number of reasons. Initially, with funding in place, downtown merchants requested a construction delay, as they did not desire the streets to be torn up during the 1980 Christmas shopping season. Their request was accepted by the Metropolitan Planning Organization (MPO), an entity that assigns priorities for the use of state and federal funds in street and highway projects. However, the MPO then transferred the monies intended for the Hemming Plaza Pedestrian Mall into the construction of a railroad overpass for University Boulevard near Philips Highway. In July 1981, a portion of Laura Street was closed to allow the Jacksonville Electric Authority to place electrical conduit and cable underground in anticipation of the project, which was expected to have its funding available a month later. However, the MPO viewed the completion of the plaza as a lower priority, favoring the transfer of funds to the widening of 103rd Street in Jacksonville's Westside.

Nevertheless, even with the grand Hemming Plaza revitalization plan being delayed, by the 1980s, the things that made grand department stores like May-Cohens urban trendsetters became their downfall. The first major department store to shutter its downtown Jacksonville operation was Sears. In 1972, its "Cadillac" store was the leading location in volume of sales in the retail chain's thirteen-state Southeast territory. However, with four levels and a basement that needed pumps operating 24/7 to keep water out, it was also one of the chain's most expensive to operate and maintain. In addition, the systematic destruction of downtown's economic base (relocation of maritime and railroad activities) in the 1950s and '60s eventually led to the closing of downtown's major hotels in the early 1970s. This, coupled with a recession and a new Sears at the Orange Park Mall drawing suburban customers away, led company consideration in closing the downtown store in the late 1970s. That opportunity would come in 1981.

With the chance to open in what was then the city's premier shopping mall, Sears made the decision to close the downtown store and open a 218,000-square-foot store at Regency Square Mall. According to Benard Datz, Sears store manager, "The day of the big department stores is gone until we get more people living downtown." On the other hand, Regency Square Mall had become one of the most successful shopping centers in the country. Due to this success, Martin and Joan Stein were in the process of implementing plans to spend $100 million on the expansion of the mall and construction of new development surrounding it. The Steins' development projects included the Regency Executive Office Park, Regency Lakes Apartments, a high-rise office tower and a 500,000-square-foot mall expansion on the west side of May-Cohens. Completed in 1981, Sears' new store became the $35 million west wing's main anchor. As part of the expansion project, May-Cohens' Regency Square branch was enlarged into a 147,000-square-foot operation. It became a walk-through anchor, connecting the original mall with the new addition. In addition to Sears, Rosenblum's also vacated downtown Jacksonville's Hogan Street corridor in 1981. Rosenblum's had already shuttered its stores at Regency Square and Roosevelt Malls when it decided to close its two-story, 36,000-square-foot downtown location. "To keep the business in the family, we have decided to

A view of the main entrance to May-Cohens and the St. James Building during the reconstruction of Hemming Plaza and Duval Street. *Courtesy of the Library of Congress.*

close the downtown store and concentrate our efforts on our fine Lakewood store on the Southside," Sheldon Rosenblum expressed. "There we will offer the same quality lines of men's and ladies' apparel in as broad a selection as before." According to Sheldon's older brother, Herman Rosenblum, abandoning downtown Jacksonville was a painful decision: "It is difficult to pull up our roots and move from this area. But when a substantial offer came to buy our leasehold for this building it became a good time to make a decision we were going to have to make someday soon. We can't work forever and we can't stay in business here without watering down the quality of our service."

By 1982, annual retail sales reported in downtown Jacksonville had declined to $92 million, slightly down from $94 million in 1963. On the other hand, retail sales had increased in Arlington alone due to Regency Square Mall, from $29.2 million in 1967 to $319.3 million in 1982.

More doom and gloom surrounding the Big Store would follow with the abrupt closure of the Holiday Inn City Center. The 387-room Holiday Inn City Center had opened on April 7, 1980, in the former Robert Meyer Hotel tower. The result of $10 million in renovation improvements by an investment group that included local developer Preston Haskell, the complex included Old Orleans gourmet restaurant, the Big Apple Lounge, Palm Beach Café, a one-thousand-person-capacity ballroom and meeting rooms. The 11 meeting rooms were named after U.S. cities such as Boston, San Francisco and Denver. Employing a staff of 225, the new hotel had been designed for the business traveler and convention guest. Holiday Inn City Center superintendent of services Melvin Copeland said, "There's a vast difference in this new hotel. It's better arranged. The lobby is larger and better furnished. The whole thing is more suitable for today's traveling public." According to Mayor Jake Godbold, the hotel was "a much-needed boost in the revitalization of downtown Jacksonville" by providing a boost in area employment and $150,000 in annual ad valorem taxes. Unfortunately, citing significant losses, downtown's only major hotel ended up closing less than two years after its grand opening. With this depressing news, Mayor Godbold said the hotel closing pointed to the importance of moving forward with the development of a convention center for downtown Jacksonville.

When the Holiday Inn City Center shut down on July 7, 1982, 150 employees were laid off and $200,801 in annual tax revenue was lost, creating dim prospects of the Big Store's long-term survival. In response to the Holiday Inn City Center's closing, May-Cohens president Robert B. Cockayne said that the hotel's fate was a "clear sign that they've [city officials] got to stop horsing around and do something about downtown development." For Cockayne, it was either that or no future for the city and the Big Store. That same day, Cockayne made it publicly known that the once-prestigious Big Store, housed in the Henry J. Kluhto–designed St. James Building, was being considered for closing and that a final decision would be made within six months. "We've been operating at a break-even point or less for several years. It's been obvious to us for some time that something had to be done," proclaimed Cockayne.

At the time, May-Cohens had recently completed a seven-month study to determine what to do with the future of the downtown flagship store, which employed 250 people. These options included closing the store outright, relocating to another downtown location or reducing the amount of space used by the department store in the building, something nearby Ivey's had done in recent years. This option revolved around the idea that the department store would be consolidated to the first two floors, allowing the top two floors to be leased as office space. May-Cohens believed that there was an opportunity for the city to consolidate its offices in the portion of the St. James Building that wasn't suitable for continued use as retail.

While the future of the Big Store was unknown, Cockayne concluded that one thing was for certain: "If we stay, we've got to make more efficient use of our space. Right now, we operate our Regency Square store with less than one-third of the space we have here, and that store is very profitable."

Despite the lost optimism and closure of the Holiday Inn City Center and downtown's second-largest department store, May-Cohens and the remaining downtown department stores waited as long as they could for city leaders to finally live up to the promise of revitalizing downtown Jacksonville. In October 1982, Cockayne stated that the company planned to remain downtown, the Big Store's business was growing and his earlier comments were taken out of context: "I made that statement in reference to a worst-case situation: if the situation deteriorated more rapidly and deeply, then we may close downtown. It is always a possibility, as anything is a possibility, but it is a remote possibility. The way things are now, we plan to be downtown."

However, September's announcement of another enclosed mall coming to Jacksonville signaled that more competition for the Big Store and the surrounding downtown retail market was on the way. "When complete, this mall will employ the newest concepts in suburban shopping facilities. It's going to be something very unique, architecturally. It's not going to be the size of a major mall. It will be 25 to 40 percent of an Orange Park Mall," said Kennon G. Holmes, Haskell Company senior vice-president for project development.

Developed by Clearwater-based National Capital Investments, the two-level Grande Boulevard Mall was intended to cater to the upscale retail market that had once dominated the retail scene around Hemming Park and Hogan Street. Plans were announced in September 1982. Located at the intersection of Old Baymeadows Road and Southside Boulevard in the then-booming Baymeadows section of Jacksonville, the 289,000-square-foot mall featured sixty-eight specialty shops wrapped around an 80,000-square-foot Jacobson's Department Store. Jacobson's was founded in 1838 in Reed City, Michigan, by Abram Jacobson before relocating its headquarters to Jackson, Michigan, in 1937. Reporting close to $300 million in annual sales by the end of 1982, Jacobson's catered to the upscale shopper with sophisticated tastes. Its primary targeted retail base had traditionally been the white-collar, professional, "yuppie" market. Believing itself a class above most department stores in the region, the chain considered department stores such as Nordstrom, Neiman-Marcus, Lord & Taylor and Saks Fifth Avenue as its competition. Getting Jacobson's to commit to anchor the mall was a direct result of the mall's design and scale. Jacobson's preferred to locate in malls that were smaller than traditional shopping centers. This strategy allowed it to be the dominant anchor, clustering with a contingent of complementing specialty retailers that preferred to be adjacent to it.

Grand Boulevard Mall opened a year later on November 17, 1983, with a list of high-end merchants that included John Baldwin (specialty clothing), Michael Winston (menswear), Lyon's, Pebbles, La Tierra, La Casa Ropa and the Deerwood Bootery. Completed for $16 million, National Capital Investors expected the mall to do between $225 and $250 per square foot in sales, which was twice the national average. At the time of Jacobson's entrance into the local market, May-Cohens was operating six north Florida stores with more than $65 million in sales annually.

In March 1984, downtown retailers were dealt another blow from the $14 million expansion of Orange Park Mall. This project included the addition of a 138,000-square-foot JCPenney department store, a five-hundred-seat food court and fifty specialty stores in a new wing just south of the mall's May-Cohens department store.

In addition to increased suburban competition, the slow-moving Hemming Plaza construction project hit a major snag in May 1984 when bids on its reconstruction came in about 40 percent above engineering estimates. The project, which involved the reconstruction of the streets surrounding the plaza, had been originally estimated to cost $1,766,901. However, three bids received from contractors placed the true costs between $2,473,239 and

$2,932,484. Originally anticipated to start in 1978 and take fifteen months to complete, six years of construction and indecision were beginning to have a drastic effect on the retailers surrounding the construction zone. What had been conceived of as a way to reenergize downtown retail had turned into the nightmare that would permanently put an end to the life of the remaining downtown department stores.

After forty-three years of anchoring what was once downtown's most prominent retail intersection, Furchgott's permanently shut down its seventy-thousand-square-foot flagship department store at 130 Adams Street on March 31, 1984. When this decision was made, the company mentioned it would eventually open a smaller, single-level operation in the five-story building. However, those plans also failed to materialize. On July 31, 1984, only four months later, another longtime downtown institution ceased operations as Levy-Wolf closed its store after fifty-seven years of being in business two blocks south of the Big Store. Founded in 1912 as Levy's, the department store had been purchased by national clothing manufacturer Hart Schaffner & Mark in July 1964. Hart Schaffner & Mark had also recently acquired Harold F. Wolf's nearby Wolf Brother's men's clothing store at 211 West Adams Street. In 1969, Hart Schaffner & Mark consolidated operations by closing the Wolf Brother's store and renaming Levy's Levy-Wolf. Remembering Levy-Wolf, Jacksonville attorney William Nussbaum recalled, "In Levy's, the ladies could purchase fur coats, mink, sable, etc. I'll bet you can't find such a coat for sale within 100 miles of here today."

In January 1985, Furchgott's, Inc. filed for protection from creditors under Chapter 11 of the United States Bankruptcy Code. Initially, Jacksonville-based Stein Mart agreed to buy the company. However, this deal fell apart when Schroder Center Management Inc. of Dallas, Texas, the managers of Regency Square Mall, refused to allow Stein Mart into the shopping center. Stein Mart then formed a joint venture with Body Shops of America to buy the company but was outbid by a Dallas-based real estate company owned by Dean Hoover on April 30, 1985. To make that purchase, Hoover borrowed money from Regency Square's owners, Schroder Center Management, Inc. of Dallas. One week later, on May 8, 1985, the financially troubled chain's three remaining stores in Regency Square, Roosevelt Square and Orange Park Malls abruptly closed their doors for good, eliminating 125 sales positions and putting the final nail in the coffin of Jacksonville's oldest department store after 116 years of continuous operation.

The negative trend would continue, with the summer of 1985 delivering a crushing blow to the chances of a retail revival for downtown's department stores. Already losing the battle to continued growth and popularity of Jacksonville's shopping malls, downtown's stores also were dealing with the slow-moving construction around Hemming Plaza and stricter enforcement of parking regulations in the area. In September 1984, months earlier, the reconstruction of the streets surrounding Hemming Plaza had finally begun. The goal of the project was to level out the entire area, creating an environment where the streets and plaza would be on the same level with bollards, which were decorative movable barriers intended to separate pedestrian and vehicular traffic. Unfortunately, the $2.5 million streetscape project would require the closure of Duval, Laura and Monroe Streets for fifteen months, making it difficult for the public to access the Big Store and its neighboring department stores.

By the summer of 1985, two of the Big Store's struggling neighbors decided to throw in the towel in favor of abandoning downtown and refocusing on the growth of their suburban branches. On June 24, 1985, after claiming their businesses were struggling and customer traffic dwindling, both Ivey's and JCPenney announced plans to close their downtown stores, leaving the Big Store surrounded by two large vacant shells. "It's because of declining sales. It's just that we feel the business is going to the suburbs," said Raymond Cole, Ivey's vice-president of sales promotion.

By this time, the downtown Ivey's store's top three levels had already been mothballed, reducing the store's overall square footage to eighty-nine thousand square feet spread over three levels. In a prepared release statement, Ivey's president and chief executive officer, Stanley Zweck-Bronner, proclaimed, "As the growth of the downtown business community has developed south towards the river, the Laura and Church Streets location has become less convenient. It is unfortunate that the era of our downtown store must end, but it is clear that the majority of customers prefer the convenience of our newer stores." According to Cole, Ivey's had known for some time that this day would come, and it had already prepared to offer its employees comparable positions at its Roosevelt, Regency and Orange Park Mall locations.

While Ivey's ceased operations at 43 West Church Street on July 13, 1985, JCPenney intended to remain open through the Christmas season, officially closing its store at 320 North Hogan Street on December 28, 1985. However, by August, JCPenney had changed its mind by advancing the closing date to October 26, 1985. "The shifting shopping patterns in the downtown area have hurt sales and it's difficult for the stores to achieve acceptable profit levels," said Dan Unger, district manager for JCPenney in Jacksonville.

"Basically, we decided it would be easier to take care of our associates before the peak holiday season, rather than afterwards." Upon closing, the company offered its downtown employees the opportunity of being transferred to its remaining suburban locations at Regency Square Mall, Orange Park Mall, Gateway Center and Cedar Hills Shopping Center. Abruptly, two of the three major anchors of the Hemming Plaza redevelopment plan were gone, leaving May-Cohens' Big Store all alone.

Upon hearing the news of JCPenney's and Ivey's departures, Larry Hazouri, owner of the Desert Rider Sandwich Shops, said, "I'm shocked. It looks like that's the last blow for the big downtown merchants. I wouldn't be surprised to see May Cohens go next." At the time, Jan Ladnier, vice-president of sales at the Big Store, responded that the downtown store was alive and well. According to Ladnier, "The renovation of Hemming Plaza has hurt but we're hoping that things will turn around when all that construction is completed."

Finally, on July 26, 1986, Mayor Jake Godbold, a white-faced mime, a comedian, rock music, multicolored balloons and a crowd of four hundred welcomed the reopening of Hemming Park, which was now rebranded

The Big Store as seen from Hogan Street during the reconstruction of Duval Street. *Courtesy of the Library of Congress.*

Hemming Plaza. The centerpiece of the downtown redevelopment plan developed fifteen years earlier was complete.

Since October 1984, one street or another around Hemming Plaza had been torn up for the long-awaited reconstruction of Laura, Hogan, Monroe and Duval Streets. Merchants waited for years to see these once-busy downtown streets transformed into the pedestrian-oriented mall with the plaza as its centerpiece. Now, that day had finally arrived. Unfortunately, during the implementation of the project, JCPenney, Ivey's, Levy-Wolf and Furchgott's had all closed, leaving the Big Store as the only major department store in downtown Jacksonville still operating.

In 1986, to address changing market conditions and retail trends, May-Cohens reduced the size of the Big Store by moving most of its second-floor merchandise to the first floor, allowing the second floor to be used as a bargain basement. In February 1987, the store removed the furniture and home decorating departments from the third floor, relegating a few items to the first-floor's mezzanine. Still struggling to maintain a viable existence in a building over 300,000 square feet, the company reduced the store's footprint to one level by mothballing the basement and third floor and using the second floor a few days a month.

May-Cohens' efforts to reduce the massive Big Store to a single level didn't exactly inspire public confidence in its chances for survival. By early March 1987, public predictions were already being made that the store would not make it through the end of the year. That month, the *Jacksonville Business Journal*'s George Wachendorf, believing the store was a victim of anemic sales caused by shoppers shifting to the suburbs, wrote an editorial predicting the Big Store's demise:

> *If you like safe predictions, I have a couple. The first is that May Cohens will be out of downtown Jacksonville by the end of the year. The second is that the departure of the department store, which already has downsized its operations to main floor and mezzanine, will give most of us a knee-jerk "ain't it awful" reaction.*
>
> *The departure merely will be a confirmation of an unavoidable change in the character of the downtown business district here and in most other cities around the country. Where large core-city residential populations do not exist, downtowns have ceased to function as centers for basic shopping.*

Wachendorf's prediction would come true four months later. Despite company executives' attempts to do everything possible to keep the store's doors open, time finally ran out for the Big Store that Jacob Cohen had built in 1912. The announcement of May-Cohens' closure to the downtown flagship store's sixty-one sales employees occurred at a 9:30 a.m. meeting on July 27, 1987, one month after the opening of the Jacksonville Landing six blocks away. "The decision to close the downtown store was made due to its declining productivity and the shift of retail patterns toward the river and the suburbs," said Thomas J. Hogan, May-Cohens president and chief executive officer. Hogan had recently replaced Robert Cockayne as the company's president after Cockayne transferred to a May Company subsidiary in Cleveland, Ohio. According to Hogan, the company would focus its merchandising efforts on its other stores and remain committed to continuing to offer customers the quality merchandise and service they had grown to expect.

The same day as the announcement of the downtown store's closure, Jacksonville mayor Tommy Hazouri revealed plans for a $90 million, forty-one-story tower for the headquarters of Barnett Bank two blocks south of Hemming Plaza. Hazouri proclaimed, "You lose one and gain another. It's sad for Jacksonville."

Although the writing was already on the wall for the once proud Big Store, not all agreed with May-Cohens' decision to shutter downtown's last remaining department store. "Think of everything nasty to say and put my name to it," said Doug Ganson, president of the Downtown Merchants Association. Ganson believed that May-Cohens should have informed other downtown merchants that the store would cease operations at an earlier stage. Ganson stated, "Everybody is glad it's finally over. May Cohens has taken a lot out of this community, and the way it handled the closing was irresponsible."

In addition, some others stubbornly felt that the store's closing was not an indictment on the health of downtown Jacksonville's retail sector. According to Scott Adams, the deputy director of Downtown Development Authority, "If May Cohens announces their closing, it doesn't mean there is a weakness in downtown as a retail market."

Despite shuttering the Big Store, sixty years still remained on the building lease owned by St. Louis–based May Company. In addition to the department store, the May Company's May-Cohens of Florida division's headquarters was also housed in the Hemming Park building. With five stores still in operation and a sixth on the way at the Southside's proposed Avenues Mall, the company initially retained the building for its two-hundred-employee headquarters.

The main entrance of the Big Store after its 1987 closure. *Courtesy of City of Jacksonville Historic Preservation Office.*

Developed as a joint venture between CBL & Associates and Edward J. DeBartolo Corporation, the $100 million Avenues Mall shopping center was intended to become Jacksonville's largest, covering over 1.3 million square feet. In addition to a new May-Cohens, other anchors originally proposed at the center included JCPenney, Sears and Dillard's. When it opened in October 1990, over twenty-five thousand people came out to see the 140-store, two-level shopping center for themselves.

In September 1987, the remaining five May-Cohens department stores were rebranded as May Florida. The name change was intended to help the chain more closely identify with its parent corporation. According to Jan Ladnier, senior vice-president of sales promotions in 1987, "It will probably take us a year to get it [the May-Cohens name] out of the system completely. Otherwise, everything remains the same."

However, less than a year later in June 1988, May Department Stores abandoned Jacksonville by selling the five-store May Florida Stores, Inc. to Maison Blanche for $62 million. The deal allowed May to rid itself of its smallest division while exposing Maison Blanche to the lucrative Florida retail market. As a result, 325 May Florida employees were laid off from the corporate office at the St. James Building and the company's distribution center on the Westside. The remaining 995 May Florida employees were retained. May would eventually be purchased by Federated Department Stores, and all of its remaining outlets were renamed Macy's in 2005.

Industry experts suspected a deal was in the making when Thomas J. Hogan, May Florida president, who had been with May Florida for more than twenty years, left in April 1988 to assume the same role at O'Neil's, a May Department Stores subsidiary in Ohio. Prior to this deal, sales for the six May Florida stores had risen 18.5 percent, from $67.5 million in 1983 to $80 million in 1986, the year before the downtown store closed. However, the May Florida division only accounted for a tiny portion of the $10.3 billion in annual sales recorded by May Department Stores. The acquisition of the remaining May Florida stores was the second deal in the previous twelve months between Maison Blanche and May. In August 1987, May Department Stores sold the ten-store Robinson's of Florida chain to Maison Blanche.

Baton Rouge–based Maison Blanche was founded in 1897 by German immigrant Isidore Newman and was best known for introducing Mr. Bingle, a Christmas mascot, at its landmark flagship store on Canal Street. While the May Department Store chain had grown to 3,059 stores, Maison Blanche was a much smaller chain, only featuring 7 stores in Louisiana and 10 in Florida.

July 28, 1988

To our fellow Associates:

Soon each of us will be scattering around the country, embarking on new segments in our careers. At this time we would like to thank you for your dedication, hard work, professionalism and adherence to solid business principles. It was because of you that May Florida became a successful model-setting retail company.

We have all experienced the exhilaration of continually exceeding our plans and our expectations and we had a lot of fun in the process. This is how we will remember you.

Thanks again for giving that extra 10 percent that continually put us over the top.

Best of luck in whatever endeavor you undertake.

Your Senior Management Committee,

Richard Doran — William Sander

Loretta Kaplan — Max Jones

Paul Dougherty — Art Snoznik

Jon Ladnier

mayflorida

An autographed letter from senior management to May Florida employees wishing them well after the decision to sell the chain to Louisiana-based Maison Blanche in 1988. *Courtesy of Mike Field.*

One of the first moves Maison Blanche made with the May Florida chain after finalizing its purchase was shuttering the ten-year-old Gateway Center location in October 1988. Enjoying a brief renaissance after being acquired by Toronto-based Bramalea Limited, which invested $2 million in cosmetic improvements, the mall continued to decline due to changing economic and demographic factors beyond its control. The first major change came in 1985 with the closure of Jefferson Ward, a discount version of Montgomery Ward, which was quickly replaced with Zarye department store in 1986. Maison Blanche delivered the mall's second major blow. Upon entering the Jacksonville market, with annual sales of only $4 million, the Gateway store simply didn't fit the Louisiana-based company's desired demographics. According to James W. Lowe, Maison Blanche's vice-president of the Jacksonville/Daytona Beach region at the time, "The Gateway store was a marginally profitable store at best." Maison Blanche's decision would send Jacksonville's first regional mall into a downward tailspin and quick death, resulting in the shopping center's last major store, JCPenney, leaving in 1992. Sales at the store had fallen 15 percent annually since 1987, and despite an offer of free rent to stay at Gateway, JCPenney declined, choosing to relocate to the intersection of Lem Turner Road and Dunn Avenue. According to Dan Unger, JCPenney's district manager in 1992, "The lease was not the determining factor. The fact was, Gateway was no longer a viable shopping center."

While Maison Blanche closed the Gateway May Florida branch store, it moved forward with May Florida's proposed $24 million store at the Avenues Mall. On September 24, 1990, the two-story, 180,000-square-foot Avenues Mall store opened, becoming the twenty-fourth in the Maison Blanche chain. Being the first store to be newly constructed by Maison Blanche in the region, it was intended to impress, according to then-manager Lew Clipp. He said, "It's different in design, in upscale fashion fixtures. The whole store is conveying upscale. There's enough marble to build the Taj Mahal."

Maison Blanche also invested between $7 million and $9 million in each remaining May Florida store for renovations and face-lifts.

Despite shutting down stores that didn't fit Maison Blanche's demographics, the acquisition of May Florida signaled the downfall of Maison Blanche, and the rapid expansion coupled with an oil-related recession in Louisiana proved to be too much for the company to manage. In 1991, this resulted in financially strapped Maison Blanche selling eight west and central Florida stores to Dillard's, leaving it with eight Louisiana stores and eight Florida stores. Founded in 1938 by William T. Dillard and based out of Little Rock, Arkansas, the chain had acquired several department stores during

A 2012 view of the interior of the former May Florida department store at Gateway. *Courtesy of the author.*

Now a Belk, when it opened in 1990, Maison Blanche's Avenues Mall store was intended to be a cut above the former May-Cohens/May Florida stores the chain had acquired in 1988. According to then manager Lew Clipp, there was enough marble in it to build the Taj Mahal. *Courtesy of the author.*

the previous decade, vastly expanding its chain by fifty-nine branch stores throughout the southwest and southeast United States. By the 1990s, the chain had targeted expansion in Florida by purchasing Charlotte-based J.B. Ivey & Company, which included twenty-three stores in the state.

Maison Blanche itself was purchased by Mercantile Stores Inc. in February 1992 as a 16-store unit. Based out of Fairfield, Ohio, Mercantile owned and operated 102 fashion apparel stores and 16 home fashion stores in seventeen states and under thirteen different nameplates: Bacons, McAlpin's, Lion, Root's, Gayfers, J.B. White, Castner Knott, The Jones Store Company, Joslins, Hennessy's, de Lendrecie's, Glass Block and Maison Blanche. With the acquisition of Maison Blanche, all former May Florida branch stores were rebranded under the Gayfers nameplate. Gayfers was a regional department store chain that had been founded in Mobile, Alabama, in 1879 by C.J. Gayfer. During the 1950s, like May Department Stores had done with Cohen Brothers, Mercantile Stores had acquired Gayfers and then worked to expand the regional chain.

The remaining former May Florida stores operated under the Gayfers moniker for only six years before Mercantile Stores was acquired by Dillard's in 1998. While this purchase expanded Dillard's footprint into several new markets across the country, it created overlap in Jacksonville. Because of Dillard's acquisition of the J.B. Ivey & Company, both Gayfers and Dillard's (former Ivey's locations) were anchors in the Avenues and Orange Park Malls. In addition, Dillard's had already moved forward with the construction of a 200,000-square-foot store at Regency Square Mall to replace a smaller Ivey's branch store at that shopping center.

In response, Dillard's decided to sell overlapping stores to competing department store chains. Through the summer of 1998, officials from Belk, Proffitt's and Burdines were among the suitors evaluating the golden opportunity to enter a large retail market instantly with multiple stores. At the time, Proffitt's operated more than 230 department stores under chains including Parisian, McRae's, Younkers, Herberger's and Carson Pirie Scott. Miami-based Burdines, which operated nearly 50 Florida-themed department stores, had an interest in expanding into the Jacksonville market for several years.

On July 14, 1998, Dillard's announced that the four Gayfers department stores, all formerly associated with the defunct May Florida chain, would become part of seven stores traded to Belk. In return, Belk would give nine of its stores in Virginia and Tennessee to Dillard's. Like its competitor, J.B. Ivey's & Company, Belk had been based out of Charlotte, North Carolina.

Founded in 1888 by William Henry Belk, the first store was called New York Racket and then Belk Brothers after Belk's brother Dr. John Belk became his partner.

By this time, Roosevelt Mall had been acquired for $4.25 million by Atlanta-based Dewberry Capital Corporation, which was in the process of a $25 million redevelopment of the mall into an open-air shopping center. According to shopping center owner John Dewberry, the announcement was fabulous news for the center, which had been anchored by Gayfers and Stein Mart: "We're delighted to have Belk as a tenant."

Others in the community speculated on why Dillard's decided to deal with Belk instead of Burdines, which had more name recognition in Florida. According to Eric Gordon, director of the University of Florida's retailing center, "It's possible that they see Belk as further behind on the development scale than Burdines. They might rather see a Belk across the mall than a Burdines, which everybody knows about."

Despite already operating stores in St. Augustine, Brunswick and St. Mary's, the swap would allow privately held Belk to enter Jacksonville and reenter the Columbia, South Carolina market. However, the former May Florida/Gayfers store at Volusia Mall in Daytona Beach was rebranded into a Dillard's.

With its purchase, Belk expanded the Regency Square Mall store to 188,000 square feet as part of its $15 million renovation program. In addition, Belk added a Home Store department at Orange Park Mall and revamped the cosmetic department at the Avenues store. With the conversion of the former May Florida branch stores at Roosevelt, Regency Square, Orange Park and Avenues Malls into Belk operations, Belk decided to relocate its Southern Division Regional Headquarters from Gainesville to Jacksonville's Southside in 1999. According to Bud Bergren, chairman of Belk's Southern Division Regional Headquarters at the time, Jacksonville was the second-largest city that the company did business in behind Charlotte. In addition, the company was attracted by the area's economic growth and opportunities to expand Belk's market share. Employing 126 people, the Southern Division Regional Headquarters oversaw Belk's 225 stores, including all 19 of its Florida stores.

What had been a Jacksonville tradition and recognizable name for 121 continuous years had undergone several changes in the final decade of the twentieth century. Today, things have appeared to stabilize. Excluding the Big Store, which closed in 1987, and the Daytona Beach store, the four remaining original May Florida/May-Cohens branch stores continue to operate to this day as Belk's.

The department store created several of North America's first large businesses and even gave birth to the modern shopping center. What Cohen Brothers did for Jacksonville was no exception to the rule. Before 1987, life in downtown Jacksonville without Cohen Brothers' Big Store was simply unthinkable. Under the leadership of Jacob Elias Cohen, Cohen Brothers emerged at a time and place in history as a result of mass urbanization and the concentration of people in Jacksonville's centralized downtown core. Cohens spent 122 continuous years in downtown and 75 at Hemming Plaza. Generations of Jaxons grew up with the Big Store being the epicenter of downtown's vibrant retail district. While many businesses have opened and closed, the Big Store wasn't just a store—it was a downtown institution.

Chapter 11

A New Lease on Life

The closure of May-Cohens' Big Store instantly created lingering effects for the surrounding retail environment. When the Big Store ceased operations, many people assumed the entire building had closed. However, the structure was originally designed by Henry J. Klutho as a mixed-use building. Despite May-Cohens' departure, there were still as many as nineteen tenants operating on the St. James Building's fourth floor. These tenants included dentists, a podiatrist and polygraphists. One tenant, Palmer's Beauty Shop, had been an occupant of the building since 1937. Palmer's manager, Mrs. McNeil, demanded they'd have to kick her out before she'd leave. However, after fifty-one years of leasing space in the St. James Building, Palmer's closed its fourth-floor salon in 1988. By 1989, there were only a handful of businesses still occupying the fourth floor, and by 1991, the entire building had been vacated.

At the time of the store's closure, seven years remained on the long-term lease of the department store space that was agreed upon when the May Company acquired Cohen Brothers in 1959. Two days after May-Cohens ceased its downtown operation, St. James Realty & Investment Company, the St. James Building's landlord, notified the parent company of May-Cohens that it was in default of the lease because of its action to close the store. While May-Cohens had ceased retail operations in the building, May Department Stores sublet the property to another company subsidiary, May Centers, Inc.

By the end of August 1987, May Department Stores had filed a suit against St. James Realty, claiming it was allowed to sublet all or part of its space in the building if net sales had fallen below $15 million. Although the lease required May to operate a department store in the building, it also mentioned that whoever sublet the space could use it for any purpose, allowing the department store operation to cease. Based on that, it was May's view that neither the subleasing company nor May would be required to pay rent based on a percentage of sales.

In September 1987, Councilwomen Ginny Myrick and Sandra Darling proposed moving Jacksonville City Hall into the building. While that idea was gaining traction in the community, the St. James Realty & Investment Company won its court battle with May Department Stores, gaining total control of the building by March 1989. However, by that time, May had already sold the entire May-Cohens/May Florida chain to Maison Blanche and shut down all of its Jacksonville-based operations.

In 1993, reports surfaced that Montgomery Ward & Company desired to purchase the abandoned building for its headquarters, but no deal was ever finalized. However, in December 1992, Mayor Ed Austin announced his intentions to turn the historic St. James Building into Jacksonville's new city hall, with the intention of using this project as a method to launch the revitalization of downtown. Estimated to cost $20 million to buy and renovate the building, Austin's plan was to shift thousands of city workers from the East Bay Street riverfront city hall complex to the heart of downtown, allowing the city to sell the valuable riverfront property to private development. In February 1993, the Downtown Development Authority purchased the St. James Building for $3.5 million. During a March 1993 tour of the abandoned Big Store, Mayor Austin reminisced about the store he had shopped at before it closed. "I used to buy chocolate-covered strawberries over there," Austin remarked to reporters on the media tour. To fund the project, Austin included the proposal as part of his $238.5 million River City Renaissance bond issue. An additional $500,000 in funding came in the form of a historic grant from the State of Florida.

In September 1993, the city council gave official approval of Austin's River City Renaissance, which included $20 million for the St. James Building's renovation. The reconstruction of the 345,000-square-foot historic landmark was undertaken as a joint venture between the Auchter Company and Perry-McCall Construction. Saxelbye, Incorporated was the architectural firm commissioned for the project. Designs for the facility called for the restoration of Klutho's long-lost atrium and octagonal skylight in the center of the building. A 348-seat theater-style city council chamber was laid out where storefronts had once graced Hemming Park on the first

A 2012 view of the restored central atrium and skylight in the St. James Building. *Courtesy of the author.*

Now city hall, a modern view of the St. James Building from the intersection of Laura and Duval Streets on the eve of the one-hundred-year anniversary of the Big Store's grand opening. *Courtesy of the author.*

floor. Passenger elevators featured cherry wood interiors, with pieces of the building's original elevators serving as decorative pieces. Plans also included the relocation of a number of city departments to floors where millions of Jaxsons once shopped. Consumer Affairs, a Procedure & Supply Copy Center, a media lab and the Information Technology Department would be housed on the former Big Store's mezzanine level. The Council Auditor, Disabled Services, Community Services, Adult Services, Code Enforcement and Environmental Protection/Air Quality/Water were laid out for placement on the second floor. The third floor would house offices for the Budget, Procurement & Supply, Jacksonville Human Relations Commission and Public Information Departments. Offices for the city council, general council and mayor were planned for the fourth floor.

In October 1993, the city officially purchased the building for $2.4 million, but asbestos removal increased the project's costs by $5 million. After nineteen months of renovation, 620 city employees began moving into the restored St. James Building on December 1, 1997. In a brochure developed for the building's December 12, 1997 grand opening, Mayor John Delaney stated:

> *Dear Friend: Welcome to your new City Hall—the beautiful St. James Building at Hemming Plaza! The refurbished St. James Building is a masterpiece of architecture, rich in folklore and history. For more than 50 years, the building served as the center of commerce for downtown Jacksonville. Now, in its second life, the St. James Building is the centerpiece of our consolidated city government.*

Chapter 12

Remembering the Big Store

In October 2012, the St. James Building that housed the Big Store will celebrate its 100th anniversary. Today, Klutho's Prairie School masterpiece has been restored to serve as Jacksonville City Hall. However, despite the Cohen name leaving the building twenty-five years earlier, the memories of the Big Store and the retail environment it created still remain in the hearts of people who came to downtown to work, shop and play.

In 1996, nearly a decade after the Big Store's closing, the Luggage Shop owner, Sam Bucholtz, remembers its economic and cultural impact during the holiday season. The Big Store was known for its ability to frame the Hemming Park retail district with window decorations with enough trappings to invoke the holiday spirit among the most jaded pedestrians. It even had one display window that was dedicated to showing every desirable toy imaginable. During Christmas season, the Big Store even converted its mezzanine level into a North Pole, complete with Santa and elves. According to Bucholtz, "Years ago, Cohens would take their entire second floor and turn it into a Toyland. Business was good for us then, too, so we also created expensive decorations in our windows."

For attorney William Nussbaum:

> *Cohens was a great store in its heyday. The candy counter was superb—Annaclairs, turtles, dark chocolate almond bark and so on. It had what I'm sure was the first escalator I rode on—and tried to get down the up and vice versa. It had a real half-floor mezzanine from which you could look down*

A panoramic view of Hemming Park, the Windsor Hotel and Cohen Brothers' Big Store prior to 1920. *Courtesy of the Library of Congress.*

> *onto the ground floor. And most amazing of all, it had real salespeople who would try to help you buy something you were looking for. Have you ever heard of such a thing?*

Nussbaum also recalls the Big Store's display windows being a huge holiday season attraction:

> *The huge window on the southwest corner of the building was a considerable attraction during the Christmas season. For weeks the window would be shrouded while the display was built—different every year. I suppose you could say it was a harbinger of fancy (as by Sally Industries here in town) animated puppets to come. You get the idea: Santa Claus wiggling around and saying something profound like "Ho-ho-ho." Elves. Reindeer. Toy trains running around. Furchgott's had a similar window (corner of the store on Hogan and Adams), but it was not as big as the one there on Hogan and Duval in the Big Store.*

Linda Bremer also remembers the window displays of downtown's department stores: "Furchgott's, Cohens and many other stores had such beautiful window displays and lobbies that you knew you were somewhere special when you went in the store. Mall stores never equaled that feeling." In Dorothy Fletcher's *Growing Up Jacksonville*, retired songwriter, musician and metal shop teacher Mike Johnson shared his memories of Cohens' Christmas displays:

Yes, my parents and I made special pilgrimages to the Cohens store display windows that did have animated figures, toys, running electric trains, dangling airplanes, lots of spun-glass winter-looking fluff and fake snow. Spray snow was kind of new and, for us, exotic at that time. I had to have some and, finally, cajoled enough to get a can. Some of it is probably still stuck to the windows on the old house on Redwood Avenue.

Royce Bardin, recalling his experiences with both May-Cohens and J.B. Ivey's & Company, says:

I was the last person in the Visual Merchandising Department when Ivey's closed. It was a very cool store. In the end all the top floors were closed. Brother's restaurant was on the third floor, and there was a big markdown department where all the local stores sent their drastically reduced merchandise. The exterior walls had really nice murals that were painted for the children's department, and there were a bunch of children's props from the old days living there. During my years at Ivey's, I worked in the downtown Jacksonville, Orange Park, Regency Square, Roosevelt Mall, Winter Park Mall, Colonial Plaza Mall [Orlando] *and Daytona Mall stores.*

But even cooler was downtown May-Cohens, where I also worked in display. I still don't think I got to see every little crevice and corner in that building, but I explored a lot. Cohens was a very cool store. You could buy most things you needed under one roof. And it had a cool basement. I am so glad I had the opportunity to work at Cohens, Furchgott's and Ivey's downtown. It was an experience that will never be duplicated in Jacksonville. At least not in my lifetime. During that time, even into the 1970s, there was a tremendous amount of activity on the streets, and most blocks were filled with shops and restaurants. I'm not one to live in the past, but I do miss those downtown days. If you are young or new to the area and never saw downtown when it was vibrant and it wasn't filled with empty lots, you will understand the remorse for what it has become. Let's just hope that in the very near future it will be revived, albeit into a new form. I don't pine for the good old days, but for downtown I do.

For Jennifer Hewett-Apperson, an urban and regional planner, the Big Store was a special place:

My memories stem more from the general experience and excitement of going downtown to the "fancy" department stores. I vividly remember shopping at May-Cohens and Ivey's with my mother and grandmother when I was a kid. I remember it being such a treat to go to the downtown department stores to shop. Even though we frequented the Regency Square May-Cohens, the downtown store was always more special. I think it was the experience of a standalone building that was also so beautiful. Man, do I miss the regional and local department stores. The mall stores were fine, but the downtown stores were really special—a grander experience, if you will.

For John Sullivan, the May-Cohens men's department stood out:

May-Cohens had the best men's department of any department store. They always had what I was looking for, and the staff was always helpful without being pushy. No wonder they were in business for so long. Back in the day, May-Cohens was considered expensive, but I found out with clothes you really do get what you pay for. Thanks for everything, May-Cohens. You left us way too soon.

Sullivan also recalls having breakfast with Santa as a child at May-Cohens:

When I was three years old, the downtown May-Cohens had a huge breakfast with Santa Claus event. This would have been Christmas 1969.

I remember a little bit about it, but my parents talked about it for years. They said May-Cohens did an amazing job. It rivaled Higbees in A Christmas Story. *I still have the picture of my sister and me sitting on Santa's lap, but unlike Higbees, this Santa was not evil. As I remember, after breakfast and after all the kids got to sit in Santa's lap, everyone went across the street to Hemming Park, where Santa Claus was given the key to the city by the mayor, Hans Tanzler, in the old Hemming Park band shell. Several years later, I went back to Hemming Plaza, and the band shell was gone—along with most of the park. Oh well.*

A visit to May-Cohens was a special treat for Dorothy Fletcher. In a 2009 *Florida Times-Union* editorial, she wrote:

In the '50s, I thought it a special treat to dress up in Sunday clothes and go downtown to see Daddy at his work. It always meant lunch and shopping at Cohens. My father worked for USF&G Insurance, located in what is now the vacant Physician's Building across the street from City Hall. After an audience with the boss, my family would hold hands as we crossed Hogan Street to enter what I thought was one of the most magical places in town—Cohens. Immediately, the smell of chocolates at the candy counter enveloped us—like chocolate-covered strawberries or the Milk Chocolate Annaclairs. As we moved along, we seemed to swirl through clouds of perfume in the delightfully cooled air. When at last we made it to the small café in the northwest corner, we feasted on sandwiches at little tables hardly big enough to accommodate our family of five.

The success of Jacob Elias Cohen's Big Store stimulated a downtown retail environment that included large multi-level department stores such as Sears' Cadillac store, Furchgott's and Ivey's. Combined with the Big Store, residents also shared their memories of these grand retail institutions. For several years, Sears' Cadillac store was the second-largest downtown department store, behind the Big Store.

John Christian's first credit card came from Sears:

In 1969, I was sixteen years old and had a job with Colonial Stores at Regency Square (brand-new grocery store). I had purchased a new 1969 Datsun station wagon from Obie's Datsun on Atlantic Boulevard with $500 down. All they required was a quick signature from my *mom. I rode my bicycle to the dealership and drove the car home. The next day, I drove downtown to Sears and applied for a credit card. The manager took me in his business office and interviewed me. I told him I had a job and a car and I did extra work on the weekends to earn additional money. He asked me why I wanted a credit card. I told him I wanted a three-horsepower outboard motor for my ten-foot john boat. He asked me to make a down payment and to make three additional payments while the motor was on hold and he would issue me a credit card in three months. I went back in three months, and the manager introduced me to a guy in accounting and they gave me my card. Here I was barely seventeen, had a car, a boat and job to boot. I'll never forget the professionalism and the genuine interest the manager from Sears showed me back then. It was a great store but a different time than today.*

Robert Mann thinks of sweets when he remembers the old downtown Sears store: "Downtown was *the place* to be, the scent of fresh roasted nuts in the Sears Super-Store." Attorney Mike Berry adds, "Amen on the candy and nut counter. I also remember going there in August each year to buy school clothes and being fascinated by the vacuum cleaner set up to blow and suspending a beach ball in mid-air."

Regarding J.B. & Ivey's & Company, Mann recalls, "J.B. Ivey was very good to his employees; my wife was a divisional executive at the time." The adjacent rotating "Embers restaurant was a fantastic experience. The rotation so slow as not to be noticed, but you would find yourself moving from the steak to the vegies and wow, different view outside. By the time the ice cream and cake was served, you had made a complete circle."

Sharing his memories of the J.B. Ivey's development, Mike Dreaden adds:

The big stores were already beginning to move out into the suburbs in the 1960s when Ivey's came to Jacksonville. This was at about the same time the big new Sears opened downtown. As for the revolving Embers restaurant on the top of the building, it was indeed a spectacular view. I went one time. My parents decided my brothers and I should be exposed to a fine dining experience. Up until that time, our idea of a high-end meal was the fried shrimp at Morrison's cafeteria (which, now that I think about it, I really miss!). So our family of five went to the Embers one night for dinner. Of the food I can say nothing; it has faded from my memory. What I do recall was the amazing panoramic sight of downtown, the river, the bridges and everything else moving by slowly as the restaurant turned. Almost fifty years later, my memory of the experience is vivid. Those were the days when it really felt like Jacksonville was on the move and big things were happening. Very exciting!

William Nussbaum remembers, "During the Christmas shopping season, the corner window of Furchgott's had an animated display in it that changed each year. You know, toy trains, elves wrapping presents, flying reindeer and so on." Jacksonville resident Eric Clark adds, "I remember going there as a child and even as a young adult to shop. It was always upscale and such a nice place to shop."

Royce Bardin recollects, "Furchgott's was an awesome store. I worked there in high school. As a matter of fact, Adams and Hogan Street was a very active retail intersection. Rosenblum's, Florsheim Shoes, Furchgott's and Levy-Wolf. It was a whole different city then, and on Friday nights, it was usually super busy."

Robert Mann remembers Furchgott's and its neighbor, Rosenblum's, being impressive retailers:

> *As one that enjoyed Jacksonville's downtown in the 1950s and 1960s, I'm here to tell y'all there was* nothing *mundane about Furchgott's…* ever. *Whatever their building might have lacked on the outside, they more than made up for it on the inside. Furchgott's was top shelf all the way through, every bit the equal of Sak's or Macy's, maybe even better. The interior of the "new" 1980s Regency Mall store was done in rose marble, and they had robots that wandered around, introduced themselves and made suggestions on gifts based on what you told them. Rosenblum's in that same era was the creme de la creme of the starched-collar nabob set and something of a fad for students at area high schools. "Psst…Sally got that at Rosenblum's!" was a higher compliment then "She went to Jared's." I haven't been back in one of the surviving Rosenblum's stores, but if they are anything like in the past, you can't go wrong for appearance and style, you most certainly* will *impress the boss.*

The Big Store at Hemming Park was the epitome of Jacksonville's shopping scene for nearly eight decades. Its trend-setting fashions, upscale merchandising and center-of-the-city location enshrined it as the mecca for sophisticated shopping in a rapidly growing sunbelt metropolis. Throughout

Restored to its original grandeur, the St. James Building proudly dominates Hemming Plaza in the same impressive manner that it did a century ago. *Courtesy of the author.*

history, several stores have started and ended their careers during the Cohen Brothers' magical 167-year run. All of them had the same equipment at the start except the one intangible thing that made the Big Store grow continuously—a sincere desire to give a little better service and a little better merchandise to all customers.

From the Candy Kitchen

Annaclairs

Ingredients

1 cup sugar
1 cup dark corn syrup
1 tablespoon vinegar
1 tablespoon baking soda
1 pound chocolate almond bark, melted

Directions

1. In a heavy saucepan, combine sugar, corn syrup and vinegar.
2. Cook over medium heat, stirring constantly, until sugar dissolves.
3. Cook without stirring until the temperature reaches 300° F (hard crack stage) on a candy thermometer.
4. Do not overcook.
5. Remove from the heat and quickly stir in baking soda.
6. Pour into a buttered 13x9x2" baking pan.
7. When cool, break into bite-size pieces.
8. Dip into melted chocolate; place on waxed paper until the chocolate is firm.
9. Store candy tightly covered.

Yield: 1½ pounds

Bibliography

From Germany to Jacksonville

Breiner, David, and Marion Cleaver. "Tribeca East Historic District Designation Report." NYC Landmarks Preservation Commission, December 8, 1992.

Glickstein, Natalie. "Cohen Brothers." *Jacksonville Magazine* 12, no. 4 (1975).

Peiser, Beatrice. "Pioneers of the South." *Southern Israelite* (1936): 10, 22.

Rayburn, Nancy. "Jacob Cohen." In *The History of Florida: Past & Present.* Vol. 3, 171. N.p.: Lewis Publishing Co., 1923. fl-genweb.net/archives/duval/bios/cohen_je.html.

Webb's Jacksonville Directory. New York: W.S. Webb & Company, 1878, 94

www.nyc.gov/html/lpc/downloads/pdf/reports/Tribeca_East_HD.pdf. July 29, 2012.

Growth and Disaster

Bessette, Leni, and Louis Stanton Warren. "From Our Past: Cohens Rose from Their Humble Beginnings to Retail Prominence." *Florida Times-Union*, December 9, 2006.

Bramson, Seth. "Speedway to Sunshine: The Story of the Florida East Coast Railway." Erin, Ontario: Boston Mills Press, 2003.

Cowart, John. "Yellow Jack in Jacksonville: The 1888 Epidemic." 2005. www.cowart.info/Florida%20History/YellowJack/YellowJack.htm.

Glickstein, Natalie. "Cohen Brothers." *Jacksonville Magazine* 12, no. 4 (1975).

"History of the Temple Congregation Ahavath Chesed." Congregation Ahavath Chesed website. www.thetemplejacksonville.org/wfmenucpanel/aboutus/history.

"The Lace Market." Experience Nottinghamshire. www.experiencenottinghamshire.com/the-lace-market.

Lisicky, Michael J. *Wanamaker's: Meet Me at the Eagle*. Charleston, South Carolina: The History Press, 2010.

Mitchell, Laia. "The Great Fire of Jacksonville: An Artistic Description of a Gloomy Affair." University of Florida George A. Smathers Libraries Department of Special Collections. web.uflib.ufl.edu/spec/pkyonge/jacksonville/fire.html. Digitized 28 February 2001.

Peiser, Beatrice. "Pioneers of the South." *Southern Israelite* (1936): 10, 22.

The Big Store Comes to Jacksonville

Broward, Robert C. "The Architecture of Henry J. Klutho." Jacksonville Historical Society, Jacksonville, Florida, 2003.

Florida Times-Union. "St. James Hotel, 1869–1901." December 31, 1937.

Glickstein, Natalie. "Cohen Brothers." *Jacksonville Magazine* 12, no. 4 (1975).

Harvey, David. "The History of the Windsor Hotel in Jacksonville, Florida." www.trails.com/facts_17148_history-windsor-hotel-jacksonville-florida.html.

"St. James Building Designation Application and Report." City of Jacksonville Planning & Development Department, 2001.

An Institution for the People

Bessette, Leni, and Louis Stanton Warren. "Pre-Christmas Outing in 1919 Turned Tragic at Railroad Crossing." *Florida Times-Union*, March 13, 2004.

Craig, James. "Far-Sighted Vision of Cohen's Back in 1866 Responsible for Greatly Expanded 'Big Store.'" *Florida Times-Union*, July 7, 1949.

Davis, Ennis. "The Uncovering of a Jacksonville Slaughterhouse." MetroJacksonville.com, May 31, 2012.

Florida Times-Union. "Amazing Merchandizing Idea Offered on Cohen Brothers New Third Floor; 'Built for Beauty as Well as Budgets.'" July 17, 1949.

Foley, Bill. "Millennium Moment: June 4, 1945: WWII Warning to Japan Had Jacksonville Roots." *Florida Times-Union*, June 4, 1999.

———. "New City Hall Will Never Match Big Store for Window Displays." *Florida Times-Union*, November 17, 1997.

———. "Nothing Can Erase the Past." *Florida Times-Union*, November 30, 1997.

Glickstein, Natalie. "Cohen Brothers." *Jacksonville Magazine* 12, no. 4 (1975).

The History of the Garden Club of Jacksonville, Florida. Jacksonville: Garden Club of Jacksonville, Florida, 1960.

"IN MEMORIAM—Jerrold R. Zacharias." Document from the City of Jacksonville Historic Preservation Commission Office.

Martin, Richard. "1918: The Year of the Lost Illusion." *Florida Times-Union* Centennial Edition, October 1, 1969.

The Merck Report. Vol. 13. New York: Merck & Company, 1904, 120.

Rumbarger, John. *Profits, Power, and Prohibition: Alcohol Reform and the Industrializing of America, 1800–1930.* New York: State University of New York Press, 1989.

"State Marketing Bureau." Know Florida. Issued by the State Department of Agriculture, circa 1935, 4–5.

Tamilia, Robert. "The Wonderful World of the Department Store in Historical Perspective: A Comprehensive International Bibliography Partially Annotated." May 2002. faculty.quinnipiac.edu/charm/dept.store.pdf.

A NEW NAME

Brumley, Jayne, and Joseph Crain. "May Company Operation of Cohen's Slated." *Florida Times-Union*, November 25, 1958.

Florida Times-Union. "Cohen's to Start $2 Million Renovation Program Soon." June 28, 1959.

———. "First Store of May Company Served Colorado Miners." November 25, 1958.

Foley, Bill. "JFK Were Just 2 of the Political Curiosities Here in 1960." *Florida Times-Union*, May 4, 1994.

"History of Price's Fine Chocolate History." Price's Fine Chocolates. secured.keysql.com/sweetshopusa/shop.asp?catId=28719.

Hurst, Rodney. *It Was Never About a Hot Dog and a Coke!* Livermore, CA: WingSpan Press, 2008.

Jacksonville Daily Record. "50 Years Ago This Week." May 24, 2010.

Wakefield, Vivian. "They Well Remember the Ax Handles." *Florida Times-Union*, February 25, 1995.

Weir, Nancy. "'Candy Man' Makes Smiles." *Florida Times-Union*, November 22, 1979.

GROWING UP AROUND THE BIG STORE

Levy's vertical file. City of Jacksonville Historic Preservation Office.

Marbut, Max. "Second Life for Historic Building." *Jacksonville Daily Record*, September 17, 2010.

Whitney, Dave. "Downtown Clothing Store Will Close, but the Name Carries On." *Florida Times-Union*, June 7, 1981.

Wood, Wayne. *Jacksonville's Architectural Heritage: Landmarks for the Future.* Jacksonville: University of North Florida Press, 1989.

CHANGING DEMOGRAPHICS: SUBURBAN EXPLOSION

Badger, Emily. "The Shopping Mall Turns 60 (and Prepares to Retire)." The Atlantic Cities. July 13, 2012. www.theatlanticcities.com/arts-and-lifestyle/2012/07/shopping-mall-turns-60-and-prepares-retire/2568.

Florida Times-Union. "Montgomery Ward to Build Store in Normandy Mall Shopping Center." May 19, 1963.

———. "Penney's Will Build Two Suburban Stores." November 29, 1957.

———. "Roosevelt Mall: After 20 Years, It's Still More Than Just Another Place to Shop." July 29, 1981.

———. "Southeast's Biggest Shopping Center to Be Erected Here." November 17, 1957.

The Big Store Heads to the Suburbs

Crain, Joseph. "Local Cooperation Is Praised at Regency Square Ceremonies." *Florida Times-Union*, January 6, 1965.

Parks, Cynthia. "She Put the Regal Look into Regency." *Florida Times-Union*, May 7, 1967.

A Mall for the Big Store

Carter, Susan. "Phelps Part of Downtown Fabric for 63 Years." *Jacksonville Journal*, February 17, 1986.

"Downtown VS. Suburbs." WJXT Research (1969). Study retrieved at the City of Jacksonville Public Library Special Collections Department.

Florida Times-Union. "Projections Indicating Added Downtown Jobs." November 20, 1976.

Foley, Bill. "Merchants Aiming at Big Christmas Downtown." *Florida Times-Union*, November 20, 1976.

Lissner, Michael. "JMA Goal: Put City into an Expansive Mood." *Florida Times-Union*, November 20, 1976.

Lynne Kerr, Jessie. "Park to Become a Plaza?" *Florida Times-Union*, January 30, 1970.

Moore, Judy. "Debts Forced Hotel to Close." *Jacksonville Journal*, August 13, 1977.

"The Plan for Downtown Jacksonville Report." RTKL Inc. in conjunction with Alan M. Voorhees and Associates, Inc., Gould Associates and Rivkin/Carson, Inc. September 1971.

An Icon Vanishes

Bermpohl, Charles. "City Center Hotel Checks Out." *Florida Times-Union*, July 8, 1982.

Bruner, Deborah. "May Cohens to Remain Downtown, Its President Says." *Florida Times-Union*, October 14, 1982.

Crownover, Catherine. "Belk Gets 4 Area Gayfers." *Florida Times-Union*, July 15, 1998.

———. "Burdines Might Replace Gayfers in Jacksonville." *Florida Times-Union*, June 25, 1998.

Fiorini, Philip. "May Florida Stores to Be Sold." *Florida Times-Union*, June 3, 1988.

Fish, Sandra. "May Cohens Drops 28-Year-Old Name for May Florida." *Florida Times-Union*, September 26, 1987.

Foley, Bill. "Hemming Plaza Facelift Hits Snag." *Florida Times-Union*, May 9, 1984.

Going, Norm. "Furchgott's Closes Shop." *Florida Times-Union*, May 8, 1985.

———. "Ivey's, Penney to Bid Downtown Goodbye." *Florida Times-Union*, June 25, 1985.

Goldman, Mike. "Cohens' Cockayne to Head May Chain." *Florida Times-Union*, n.d.

Jacksonville Chronicle. "Levy's Sold to Hart-S-Marx." July 3, 1964.

Jacobson Stores Inc. History. International Directory of Company Histories, Vol. 21. N.p.: St. James Press, 1998.

Kres, Mary. "New Mall at Deerwood to Bring 'New Blood.'" *Florida Times-Union*, September 22, 1982.

McTammany, Theresa. "The Avenues Makes Shopping Fashionable." Florida Times-Union, October 24, 1990.

New Orleans Times-Picayune. "Maison Blanche Plans Jacksonville Opening." September 3, 1990.

O'Reiley, Tom. "May Cohens Daring to Get Smaller." *Florida Times-Union*, March 1, 1987.

Owens, George. "New Mall's Grande Opening Set Today." *Florida Times-Union*, November 17, 1983.

Patton, Charlie. "Unfinished Plaza Criticized." *Florida Times-Union*, December 16, 1981.

Paul, Peralte. "Belk Unit Moving to Southside Building." *Florida Times-Union*, July 16, 1999.

Respess, Susan. "Downtown May Cohen's Closes; Poor Sales Blamed." *Florida Times-Union*, July 28, 1987.

Sternberg, Hans, and James Shelledy. *We Were Merchants: The Sternberg Family and the Story of Goudchaux's and Maison Blanche Department Stores*. Baton Rouge: Louisiana State University Press, 2009.

Straehley, Dayna. "Downtown Authority Already Is Working on Plans to Find May Cohens Replacement." *Jacksonville Business Journal*, July 27, 1987.

Taylor, John. "May Cohens May Close Downtown Store." *Florida Times-Union*, July 8, 1982.

Wachendorf, George. "May Cohens Seen Leaving Downtown This Year." *Jacksonville Business Journal*, March 9, 1987.

Whitney, Dave. "City Center Opening Brings Back Grand Hotel Fashion." *Florida Times-Union*, April 8, 1980.

———. "Downtown Clothing Store Will Close, but the Name Carries On." *Florida Times-Union*, June 7, 1981.

www.belk.com/media/pdf/BelkBook/BelkBookPhotosection/Belkbook_Photo_section_3_192-203_v2_m5657756983071025O.pdf

A New Lease on Life

City of Jacksonville. St. James Building brochure, December 1997, Jacksonville Historical Society.

Fallstrom, Jerry. "Mayor Visits the St. James; Nero Defends Purchase Plan." *Florida Times-Union*, March 9, 1993.

Fish, Sandra. "May Cohens Parent Sues Over St. James Site." *Florida Times-Union*, August 22, 1987.

Respess, Susan. "Tenants Want Customers to Know St. James Building Isn't Closed." *Florida Times-Union*, August 15, 1987.

Ziebarth, Jane. "Court Fight Ends Dispute on Building." *Florida Times-Union*, March 21, 1989.

Remembering the Big Store

Fletcher, Dorothy. "By the Wayside: Mercantile Magic: Cohen Brothers Department Store." *Florida Times-Union*, June 25, 2009.

Weathersbee, Tonyaa. "Hey, Santa: Remember Hemming?" *Florida Times-Union*, December 25, 1996.

About the Authors

Originally from Winter Haven, Florida, author Ennis Armon Davis graduated from Florida A&M University in 2001 with a bachelor of architecture degree and has been employed in the fields of architecture and urban planning. In 2006, he co-founded the award-winning MetroJacksonville.com, an online media entity focusing on promoting the growth of fiscally sustainable communities. He resides in Jacksonville, where he is a civic activist who has served with various organizations committed to improving urban communities, including the First Coast Section of the Florida Chapter of the American Planning Association (APA) and the Jacksonville Historical Society. He is the author of the award-winning book *Reclaiming Jacksonville*, which was also published by The History Press.

Originally from Northern Virginia, author Sarah Taylor Gojekian graduated from the University of North Florida in 2011 with a bachelor of science degree in communication—electronic media. Known as a dedicated, award-winning writer with a mind overflowing with fresh imagination, her past experience includes being the assistant news editor of the University of North Florida newspaper, the *Spinnaker*; a contributing writer for the *Sarasota Herald Tribune*; and editor for MetroJacksonville.com. In addition, she was the copy editor of the award-winning book *Reclaiming Jacksonville*, which was also published by The History Press. Working as a freelance writer, she currently resides in Atlantic Beach, where she continues to assist in the researching, production and editing of daily MetroJacksonville.com content.